HANDY SUBSTITUTIONS

NEEDED INGREDIENT	SUBSTITUTE
BAKING PRODUCTS:	
1 cup self-rising flour	1 cup all-purpose flour, 1 teaspoon baking powder, and ½ teaspoon salt
1 cup cake flour	1 cup minus 2 tablespoons all-purpose flour
1 cup all-purpose flour	1 cup and 2 tablespoons cake flour
1 cup powdered sugar	1 cup sugar and 1 tablespoon cornstarch (processed in food processor)
1 cup honey	1¼ cups sugar and ¼ cup water
1 teaspoon baking powder	¼ teaspoon baking soda and ½ teaspoon cream of tartar
1 tablespoon cornstarch	2 tablespoons all-purpose flour
1 tablespoon tapioca	1½ tablespoons all-purpose flour
EGGS AND DAIRY PRODUCTS:	
2 large eggs	3 small eggs
1 cup milk	½ cup evaporated milk and ½ cup water
1 cup plain yogurt	1 cup buttermilk
VEGETABLE PRODUCTS:	
1 pound fresh mushrooms, sliced	1 (8-ounce) can sliced mushrooms, drained, or 3 ounces dried
1 medium onion, chopped	1 tablespoon instant minced onion or 1 tablespoon onion powder
3 tablespoons chopped shallots	2½ tablespoons chopped onion and 1 teaspoon chopped garlic
SEASONING PRODUCTS:	
1 tablespoon chopped fresh herbs	1 teaspoon dried herbs or ¼ teaspoon powdered herbs
1 clove garlic	⅛ teaspoon garlic powder or minced dried garlic
1 tablespoon grated fresh gingerroot or crystallized ginger	⅛ teaspoon ground ginger
1 teaspoon ground allspice	½ teaspoon ground cinnamon and ½ teaspoon ground cloves
1 teaspoon pumpkin pie spice	½ teaspoon ground cinnamon, ¼ teaspoon ground ginger, ⅛ teaspoon ground allspice, and ⅛ teaspoon ground nutmeg
ALCOHOL:	
2 tablespoons amaretto	¼ to ½ teaspoon almond extract
2 tablespoons sherry or bourbon	1 to 2 teaspoons vanilla extract
¼ cup Marsala	¼ cup dry white wine and 1 teaspoon brandy
¼ cup or more white wine	Equal measure of white grape juice or apple juice

Lime-Marinated
Grilled Sea Bass
(recipe, page 60)

Provençal Tomato Bread Salad
(recipe, page 134)

Weight Watchers®
Cook Quick
Cook Healthy

Oxmoor House®

Library of Congress Catalog Card Number: 97-68809
ISBN: 0-8487-1648-5

Manufactured in the United States of America
First Printing 1997

Be sure to check with your health-care provider before making any changes in your diet.

Weight Watchers®, Selections®, and **POINTS**™ are registered trademarks of Weight Watchers International, Inc., and are used under license by Healthy Living, Inc.

Editor-in-Chief: Nancy Fitzpatrick Wyatt
Senior Foods Editor: Katherine M. Eakin
Senior Editor, Editorial Services: Olivia Kindig Wells
Art Director: James Boone

WEIGHT WATCHERS COOK QUICK COOK HEALTHY

Editor: Deborah Garrison Lowery
Assistant Foods Editor: Kathryn Matuszak Wheeler, R.D.
Associate Art Director: Cynthia R. Cooper
Designer: Clare T. Minges
Copy Editor: Donna Baldone
Editorial Assistant: Catherine S. Ritter
Proofreader: Kathryn Stroud
Director, Test Kitchens: Kathleen Royal Phillips
Assistant Director, Test Kitchens: Gayle Hayes Sadler
Test Kitchens Staff: Molly Baldwin, Susan Hall Bellows, Julie Christopher, Natalie E. King, Elizabeth Tyler Luckett, Jan Jacks Moon, Iris Crawley O'Brien, Jan A. Smith
Photographer: Brit Huckabay
Photo Stylist: Virginia Cravens
Publishing Systems Administrator: Rick Tucker
Production Director: Phillip Lee
Associate Production Manager: Vanessa Cobbs Richardson
Production Assistant: Faye Porter Bonner

WE'RE HERE FOR YOU!

We at Oxmoor House are dedicated to serving you with reliable information that expands your imagination and enriches your life. We welcome your comments and suggestions. Please write us at:

Oxmoor House, Inc.
Editor, *Weight Watchers*
Cook Quick Cook Healthy
2100 Lakeshore Drive
Birmingham, AL 35209

To order additional publications, call 1-205-877-6560.

Cover: Grilled Chicken Teriyaki, page 113
Back Cover: Black Forest Parfaits, page 52

CONTENTS

INTRODUCTION

WEIGHT WATCHERS QUICK & HEALTHY RECIPES

10 SECRETS

TO QUICK & HEALTHY COOKING

It's dinnertime. You want the meal to be healthy, but your family just wants to eat now! To solve this dilemma, read on for the best way to make meals quick and healthy.

1. SET UP YOUR KITCHEN FOR SPEED

When you store kitchen equipment and ingredients where you use them and in the same place everytime, you won't lose time searching for what you need.

Keep potholders, wooden spoons, pots, pans, and baking sheets as close to the oven and range as possible. Store flour, spices, mixing bowls, an electric mixer, rubber spatulas, and measuring cups and spoons near where you mix. The best place for a cutting board and knives is near the sink.

2. USE LOW-FAT CONVENIENCE FOODS

Low-fat and nonfat products have improved in flavor and texture over the past few years. Our staff recommends all of the following: low-fat and nonfat cream cheese, sour cream, and shredded cheeses; Italian-style, Mexican-style, or roasted garlic-flavored canned tomatoes; low-fat spaghetti sauces; and flavored couscous or rice mixes.

3. BUY FOOD PREPPED FOR USE

You'll get a jump start on any meal when you use shredded cabbage, packaged cut vegetables, cut vegetables from the salad bar, prewashed spinach, precooked pasta, par-boiled rice, shredded cheese, chicken strips or cubes, and trimmed and boned meat. You'll pay a bit extra for these convenience items, but it's worth it when you need to cook in a hurry.

4. READ THE RECIPE

Read the *entire* recipe before you cook. That way, if the chicken dish is served with rice, you can cook the rice while you cook the chicken. If you cook the chicken first, then discover you need cooked rice, you'll add an extra 10 to 20 minutes to the cooking time.

5. STICK TO NONSTICK SKILLETS

Thanks to the new nonstick coatings, you can get by with a teaspoon or less of vegetable oil to brown even the leanest meats. Sometimes, just a coating of cooking spray will do the trick.

6. PULL OUT THE WOK

Cooking time is a matter of minutes if the wok is hot enough before you add the meat and vegetables. Cooking quickly is great for your health as well, because there isn't time for nutrients to leach out of the food. And when you cook the meal in one dish, cleanup is a snap.

7. GET STEAMING

Steam cooking is good for speed and health. Food cooks quickly, and nutrients stay in the food instead of being lost in cooking water. To steam food, use bamboo steaming baskets or collapsible metal ones that fit inside standard pots.

8. MICROWAVE WHENEVER YOU CAN

Like steaming, microwave cooking helps vegetables retain nutrients because you cook them covered in a small amount of water.

You also can partially cook meats and casseroles in the microwave, then just finish the cooking in the oven or on the grill.

9. GRILL OUT (OR IN)

Grilling is a quick way to cook because you don't have messy pans to clean. Even more important, it's healthier because fat literally drips away from meat as it cooks.

10. DON'T DIRTY THE DISHES

Unless you love to wash dishes, use these tips to save some cleanup.
• Before you use the food processor to mix a wet or messy mixture, first chop or shred dry ingredients like nuts and cheese.
• Take a few minutes to chop extra nuts, breadcrumbs, or vegetables, and freeze them in small amounts for future use.
• Chop tomatoes right in the can with kitchen scissors.
• Measure dry ingredients before wet ones.
• Seal crackers or cookies in a heavy-duty, zip-top plastic bag, and crush them with a rolling pin.
• Marinate food in a heavy-duty, zip-top plastic bag; then throw away the bag when you're finished.

CHECK THE INDEX!

Need to make dinner in a hurry? Then turn to page 191 for help. We've listed all our SuperQuick recipes (those you can make in 15 minutes or less) on a single page. Or if you'd rather make dinner a day ahead, look for the list of Make Ahead recipes on the same page.

PLAN RIGHT TO EAT RIGHT

Whether you count Selections, calories, fat grams, or Weight Watchers new **POINTS**, follow these seven Guidelines for Healthy Living each day:

1. Consume a variety of foods.
2. Include two servings of milk products.
3. Eat at least five servings of fruits and vegetables.
4. Pay attention to serving sizes.
5. Limit refined sugars and alcohol.
6. Drink six or more glasses of water.
7. Do at least 10 minutes of physical activity.

If you use Weight Watchers Selections to plan your meals, the chart below will help you know what's right for you. Each recipe includes Selections and Bonus Calories along with a complete nutritional analysis.

LOOK FOR THE POINTS

Weight Watchers Cook Quick Cook Healthy is the first cookbook to offer **POINTS** values, an integral part of Weight Watchers new 1•2•3 Success Program. You'll find the **POINTS** per serving listed with each recipe just above the column of nutrient values.

POINTS are based on a formula for calories, fat, and fiber. Higher **POINTS** are assigned to higher calorie and higher fat foods. For instance, fruits and vegetables are low in **POINTS,** while a slice of pizza is high. (See the box below.) For more information about the 1•2•3 Success Program and the Weight Watchers meeting nearest you, call 1-800-651-6000.

FOOD *POINTS*

Broccoli	0
Carrots	0
Corn (5-inch ear)	1
Orange	1
Banana	2
Bagel (1 small)	3
Yogurt (plain nonfat)	3
Pizza (5-ounce slice)	8
Grilled cheese sandwich	13

WEIGHT WATCHERS DAILY FOOD GUIDE FOR WOMEN

FOOD CATEGORY	NUMBER OF FOOD SELECTIONS FOR YOUR WEIGHT		
	Less than 175 pounds	175 to 250 pounds	Over 250 pounds
Protein/Milk	5-6	6-7	7-8
Bread	4-5	6-7	8-9
Fruit/Vegetable	5 or more	5 or more	5 or more
Fat	2-3	3-4	4-5
Glasses of Water	6 or more	6 or more	6 or more
Bonus Calories	up to 250	up to 250	up to 250

©Weight Watchers International

appetizers
beverages

Garlic Herb Cheese Spread

TIME: PREP 12 MINUTES; CHILL 1 HOUR

SELECTIONS

FREE

POINTS

1

PER SERVING

16 CALORIES

1.1G CARBOHYDRATE

0.6G FAT (0.4G SATURATED)

0.0G FIBER

1.2G PROTEIN

2MG CHOLESTEROL

65MG SODIUM

18MG CALCIUM

0.0MG IRON

1½ cups nonfat sour cream
½ cup light process cream cheese
1 tablespoon minced fresh chives
2 teaspoons minced fresh parsley
½ teaspoon salt
½ teaspoon ground pepper
1 small clove garlic, minced, or ½ teaspoon
   minced garlic from a jar

1. Combine sour cream and cream cheese in a bowl; stir well. Stir in chives and remaining ingredients; cover and chill at least 1 hour.

2. Serve spread on bagel chips or toasted French bread, or spoon into hollowed out cherry tomatoes or mushroom caps. To store, cover cheese spread, and refrigerate up to 4 days. Yield: 2 cups (1 tablespoon per serving).

Fresh garlic and herbs make this stir-and-chill dip taste garden-fresh. The chilling time is important because it gives the flavors a chance to blend.

White Bean Dip

TIME: PREP 10 MINUTES; CHILL 1 HOUR

1	(15.8-ounce) can Great Northern beans, drained
2	teaspoons minced fresh thyme or ½ teaspoon dried thyme
2	teaspoons balsamic or red wine vinegar
1	teaspoon olive oil
½	teaspoon dry mustard
½	teaspoon ground pepper
¼	teaspoon salt
2	tablespoons minced fresh parsley

1. Combine first 7 ingredients in a medium bowl. Mash until mixture is smooth, using a potato masher; stir in parsley. Transfer to a small serving bowl; cover and chill at least 1 hour. Serve with fat free pita chips or raw vegetables. Yield: 1¼ cups (1 tablespoon per serving).

> Try other types of canned beans like black or cannellini in this recipe. Simply substitute a similar size can of your choice of beans for the can of Great Northern beans. If you don't have a potato masher, use fork tines to mash the beans.

SELECTIONS

FREE

POINTS

0

PER SERVING

16 CALORIES

2.6G CARBOHYDRATE

0.3G FAT (0.1G SATURATED)

0.5G FIBER

1.0G PROTEIN

0MG CHOLESTEROL

62MG SODIUM

10MG CALCIUM

0.4MG IRON

Baked Pita Chips

TIME: PREP 5 MINUTES; COOK 12 MINUTES

SELECTIONS
FREE

4   (6-inch) pita bread rounds
Garlic- or olive oil-flavored vegetable cooking spray

POINTS
0

1. Cut each pita round into 8 wedges; separate each wedge into 2 wedges. Place wedges in a single layer on 2 baking sheets; coat wedges with cooking spray. Bake at 350° for 12 to 13 minutes or until lightly browned. Let cool. Yield: 64 pita chips (1 chip per serving).

PER SERVING
11 CALORIES
2.0G CARBOHYDRATE
0.1G FAT (0.0G SATURATED)
0.4G FIBER
0.2G PROTEIN
0MG CHOLESTEROL
23MG SODIUM
3MG CALCIUM
0.1MG IRON

VARIATION: For Italian-flavored chips, coat pita wedges with cooking spray, and then sprinkle with ⅛ teaspoon garlic powder and ¼ teaspoon dried Italian seasoning. Bake as directed.

Experiment with your favorite seasonings for these easy homemade chips. Serve them with Garlic Herb Cheese Spread (page 10) or White Bean Dip (page 11).

Mock Pea Guacamole

2	cups frozen English peas, thawed
½	cup sliced green onions (about 2 onions)
2	tablespoons fresh cilantro
1½	tablespoons fresh lime juice
1	tablespoon salsa
¼	teaspoon salt
¼	teaspoon hot sauce

1. Position knife blade in food processor bowl. Add first 4 ingredients; process 30 seconds or until smooth, stopping once to scrape down sides. Add salsa and remaining ingredients; stir well. Serve with fat-free tortilla chips or raw vegetables. Yield: 1½ cups (1 tablespoon per serving).

Avocados, the basis of traditional guacamole, can turn brown quickly. But this mock guacamole made with English peas keeps its color, so it can be made in advance. It's a little brighter green than avocado guacamole, but it still offers a pungent southwestern kick with cilantro, salsa, and lime juice.

SELECTIONS

FREE

POINTS

0

PER SERVING

11 CALORIES

1.9G CARBOHYDRATE

0.0G FAT (0.0G SATURATED)

0.6G FIBER

0.7G PROTEIN

0MG CHOLESTEROL

44MG SODIUM

4MG CALCIUM

0.2MG IRON

Red Pepper Pesto Crostini *(photo, page 19)*

TIME: PREP 5 MINUTES; CHILL 1 HOUR

SELECTIONS

1 BREAD

POINTS

2

PER SERVING

86 CALORIES

14.7G CARBOHYDRATE

1.2G FAT (0.3G SATURATED)

0.6G FIBER

3.4G PROTEIN

2MG CHOLESTEROL

207MG SODIUM

38MG CALCIUM

0.7MG IRON

1   cup coarsely chopped, drained roasted sweet red pepper
       (about 2 peppers)
3   tablespoons freshly grated Parmesan cheese
1   tablespoon sliced almonds, toasted
2   teaspoons no–salt–added tomato paste
1   clove garlic, chopped
3   ounces nonfat cream cheese
16 (½–inch–thick) slices French bread, toasted

1. Combine first 5 ingredients in container of an electric blender; cover and process until smooth, stopping once to scrape down sides. Cover and chill at least 1 hour.

2. Spread cream cheese evenly on toast slices; top each with 1 tablespoon pepper mixture. Yield: 16 appetizers (1 per serving).

> The red pepper pesto also is delicious spooned over grilled fish, mixed with pasta, or as a sandwich spread. To make this recipe extra quick, use roasted peppers from a jar. One 7-ounce jar contains 2 roasted peppers.

Chicken Nacho Wedges

TIME: PREP 17 MINUTES; COOK 8 MINUTES

4   (8-inch) fat-free flour tortillas
Vegetable cooking spray
1   cup finely chopped green pepper
¾   cup finely chopped purple onion
1½   teaspoons ground cumin
1   (14½-ounce) can Mexican-style stewed tomatoes, undrained
         and chopped
1½   cups chopped cooked chicken breast
¼   cup minced fresh cilantro
1   cup (4 ounces) shredded reduced-fat Monterey Jack cheese

SELECTIONS

60 BONUS CALORIES

POINTS

1

PER SERVING

57 CALORIES

5.9G CARBOHYDRATE

1.4G FAT (0.6G SATURATED)

0.4G FIBER

5.2G PROTEIN

11MG CHOLESTEROL

138MG SODIUM

47MG CALCIUM

0.6MG IRON

1. Arrange tortillas on a large baking sheet coated with cooking spray; set aside.

2. Coat a large nonstick skillet with cooking spray; place over medium heat until hot. Add green pepper and onion, and cook 5 minutes or until tender, stirring often. Add cumin, and cook 1 additional minute. Add tomato; cook 3 minutes, stirring occasionally.

3. Spoon tomato mixture evenly over tortillas; top with chicken and cilantro. Sprinkle cheese evenly over chicken. Bake at 375° for 8 minutes or until tortillas are crisp. Cut each tortilla into 6 wedges. Serve immediately. Yield: 24 appetizers (1 per serving).

Chopping the stewed tomatoes right in the can with kitchen shears saves time and makes less mess.

Polynesian Marinated Drummettes

TIME: PREP 27 MINUTES; MARINATE 8 HOURS; COOK 18 MINUTES

SELECTIONS

1 PROTEIN/MILK

70 BONUS CALORIES

POINTS

3

PER SERVING

130 CALORIES

7.4G CARBOHYDRATE

4.6G FAT (1.3G SATURATED)

0.2G FIBER

13.1G PROTEIN

44MG CHOLESTEROL

268MG SODIUM

24MG CALCIUM

0.7MG IRON

3   tablespoons white wine vinegar

3   tablespoons light-colored corn syrup

3   tablespoons no-salt-added tomato paste

3   tablespoons low-sodium soy sauce

1   tablespoon minced garlic

1   teaspoon ground ginger

20 chicken drummettes (about 2½ pounds), skinned

½   cup unsweetened pineapple juice

¼   cup low-sodium soy sauce

1   tablespoon brown sugar

2   teaspoons cornstarch

1   cup low-sugar orange marmalade

1   tablespoon chopped fresh cilantro

Vegetable cooking spray

Skinning the drummettes for this recipe takes most of the preparation time. To save time, use chicken tenders. They're easy to eat and to dip in the sweet-and-sour pineapple-orange sauce.

1. Combine first 6 ingredients in a heavy-duty, zip-top plastic bag. Add drummettes; seal bag, and shake until drummettes are well coated. Marinate in refrigerator 8 hours, turning bag occasionally.

2. Combine pineapple juice and next 3 ingredients in a small saucepan. Cook over medium heat, stirring constantly, 5 minutes or until slightly thickened. Stir in marmalade and cilantro; cook over low heat until sauce is thoroughly heated.

3. Remove drummettes from marinade, discarding marinade. Place on rack of a broiler pan coated with cooking spray. Broil 5½ inches from heat (with electric oven door partially opened) 18 minutes or until done, turning once. Serve with orange marmalade mixture as a dipping sauce. Yield: 10 servings (2 drummettes and about 2 tablespoons sauce per serving).

Turkey-Asparagus Roll-Ups

TIME: PREP 11 MINUTES; COOK 2 MINUTES

6   fresh asparagus spears
1   medium carrot, scraped and cut into very thin strips
3   tablespoons nonfat cream cheese
1   tablespoon honey mustard
3   (8-inch) fat-free flour tortillas
4   ounces thinly sliced smoked turkey breast

1. Snap off tough ends of asparagus. Remove scales from stalks with a vegetable peeler, if desired.

2. Place asparagus and carrot in a large saucepan; add water to cover. Bring to a boil; cook 2 minutes or until crisp-tender. Drain and cool.

3. Combine cream cheese and honey mustard in a small bowl, stirring well. Spread evenly on top of each tortilla. Layer turkey evenly on cheese mixture. Place 2 asparagus spears 2 inches from side of each tortilla. Place carrot strips beside asparagus. Roll up tortillas, jellyroll fashion. Wrap each tortilla in plastic wrap, twisting ends to seal; chill.

4. To serve, cut each rolled tortilla into 6 pieces. Yield: 18 appetizers (1 per serving).

SELECTIONS

30 BONUS CALORIES

POINTS

1

PER SERVING

32 CALORIES

5.0G CARBOHYDRATE

0.2G FAT (0.1G SATURATED)

0.3G FIBER

2.5G PROTEIN

4MG CHOLESTEROL

130MG SODIUM

10MG CALCIUM

0.1MG IRON

When fresh asparagus is out of season, use frozen instead. Follow package directions for cooking it.

Tuna Salad Bites

TIME: PREP 14 MINUTES; CHILL 1 HOUR

SELECTIONS

30 BONUS CALORIES

POINTS

1

PER SERVING

31 CALORIES

3.3G CARBOHYDRATE

0.7G FAT (0.1G SATURATED)

0.7G FIBER

3.3G PROTEIN

5MG CHOLESTEROL

79MG SODIUM

11MG CALCIUM

0.3MG IRON

1	(6-ounce) can low-sodium, low-fat chunk white tuna in water, drained
½	cup finely chopped carrot
⅓	cup thinly sliced green onions
¼	cup sliced pimiento-stuffed olives
¼	cup low-fat mayonnaise
3	tablespoons minced fresh parsley
1	tablespoon lemon juice
½	teaspoon ground pepper
2	medium cucumbers, cut into ½-inch slices

1. Combine first 8 ingredients in a medium bowl, stirring well. Cover and chill at least 1 hour.

2. Scoop out a hollow space in center of 1 side of each cucumber slice, using a ½-teaspoon circular measuring spoon or a small melon baller. Fill centers of cucumber slices with tuna mixture. Serve immediately. Yield: 12 appetizers (1 per serving).

> For an attractive touch to these appetizers, score the peel of each cucumber lengthwise with fork tines before slicing the cucumber.

Red Pepper
Pesto Crostini
(recipe, page 14)

Strawberry-Cherry Slush
(recipe, page 22)

Black Bean Cakes

TIME: PREP 12 MINUTES; COOK 4 MINUTES

1   (15-ounce) can black beans, drained
2   tablespoons no-salt-added tomato paste
2   cloves garlic, minced
1½   teaspoons ground cumin, divided
¼   teaspoon salt
2   tablespoons fine, dry breadcrumbs
½   teaspoon ground pepper
Olive oil-flavored vegetable cooking spray
2   teaspoons olive oil
¼   cup salsa
¼   cup nonfat sour cream
Chopped fresh cilantro (optional)

1. Combine first 3 ingredients, ½ teaspoon cumin, and salt in a large bowl; mash with a fork. Divide mixture evenly into 8 balls; set aside.

2. Combine breadcrumbs, pepper, and remaining 1 teaspoon cumin in a shallow dish. Roll balls in crumb mixture. Shape into ½-inch-thick patties.

3. Coat a large nonstick skillet with cooking spray; add oil. Place over medium-high heat until hot. Add patties; cook 2 minutes on each side or until lightly browned.

4. To serve, place 1 bean cake on each of 8 individual serving plates. Top each with 1½ teaspoons salsa and 1½ teaspoons sour cream. Garnish with cilantro, if desired. Serve immediately. Yield: 8 servings.

SELECTIONS

80 BONUS CALORIES

POINTS

1

PER SERVING

79 CALORIES

12.2G CARBOHYDRATE

1.6G FAT (0.2G SATURATED)

2.0G FIBER

4.4G PROTEIN

0MG CHOLESTEROL

194MG SODIUM

29MG CALCIUM

1.2MG IRON

Garlic and cumin give these bean cakes a bold, earthy flavor.

Strawberry-Cherry Slush *(photo, page 20)*

TIME: PREP 5 MINUTES

SELECTIONS

1 FRUIT/VEGETABLE

70 BONUS CALORIES

POINTS

2

PER SERVING

120 CALORIES

29.7G CARBOHYDRATE

0.7G FAT (0.2G SATURATED)

0.6G FIBER

0.9G PROTEIN

0MG CHOLESTEROL

12MG SODIUM

18MG CALCIUM

0.7MG IRON

1⅓   cups frozen pitted sweet cherries

1   cup frozen strawberries

1   cup cherry-flavored lemon-lime soda, chilled

2   tablespoons sugar

2   tablespoons thawed frozen reduced-calorie whipped
        topping

1   tablespoon fresh lemon juice

1. Combine all ingredients in container of an electric blender; cover and process until smooth, stopping twice to scrape down sides. Pour into tall chilled glasses. Yield: 2¼ cups (¾ cup per serving).

Don't thaw the strawberries and cherries before adding them to the blender; processing the frozen berries is what makes the beverage slushy. We used cherry-flavored 7-Up for the soda, but you can substitute any other clear carbonated soda.

Cranberry-Apple Iced Tea

TIME: PREP 13 MINUTES

2	cups water
2	cranberry-flavored tea bags
1	cup cranberry-apple juice
½	cup unsweetened apple juice
2	teaspoons honey

Ice cubes

1. Bring water to a boil in a medium saucepan. Add tea bags; remove from heat. Cover and steep (let stand) 10 minutes. Remove and discard tea bags.

2. Combine tea, juices, and honey, stirring well; cover and chill. Serve over ice. Yield: 4 cups (1 cup per serving).

The fruity cranberry flavor in the tea will be stronger if you chill the beverage before pouring it over ice. Pouring hot tea over ice melts it and dilutes the tea's flavor.

SELECTIONS

1 FRUIT/VEGETABLE

POINTS

1

PER SERVING

68 CALORIES

17.4G CARBOHYDRATE

0.0G FAT (0.0G SATURATED)

0.1G FIBER

0.1G PROTEIN

0MG CHOLESTEROL

6MG SODIUM

7MG CALCIUM

0.2MG IRON

Iced Coffee Freeze

TIME: PREP 3 MINUTES

SELECTIONS

80 BONUS CALORIES

POINTS

2

PER SERVING

78 CALORIES

15.5G CARBOHYDRATE

0.1G FAT (0.1G SATURATED)

0.1G FIBER

3.7G PROTEIN

1MG CHOLESTEROL

60MG SODIUM

139MG CALCIUM

0.2MG IRON

1	cup vanilla nonfat frozen yogurt
1	cup skim milk
¼	cup strongly brewed coffee, chilled
2	tablespoons powdered sugar
1	teaspoon vanilla extract
½	teaspoon ground cinnamon
1¼	cups large ice cubes

1. Combine all ingredients in container of an electric blender; cover and process until smooth, stopping once to scrape down sides. Serve immediately. Yield: 4 cups (1 cup per serving).

Use a dark roast or a specialty coffee for a stronger taste. We suggest chocolate, amaretto, praline, and hazelnut varieties to boost the flavor.

breads

Parmesan Bruschetta

TIME: PREP 5 MINUTES; COOK 1 MINUTE

SELECTIONS

1 BREAD

POINTS

2

PER SERVING

92 CALORIES

12.8G CARBOHYDRATE

2.5G FAT (0.4G SATURATED)

0.6G FIBER

4.2G PROTEIN

7MG CHOLESTEROL

230MG SODIUM

63MG CALCIUM

0.6MG IRON

2 tablespoons grated Parmesan cheese
2 tablespoons light process cream cheese
¼ teaspoon garlic powder
¼ teaspoon dried Italian seasoning
4 (½-inch-thick) diagonally cut slices Italian bread

1. Combine first 4 ingredients in a small bowl; stir well. Spread cheese mixture evenly over bread slices.

2. Place bread slices on a baking sheet; broil 1 minute or until toasted. Yield: 4 servings (1 slice per serving).

A sharp knife with a serrated edge or an electric knife will help you cut pretty, clean slices from a fresh, soft loaf of bread.

Cranberry Scones

TIME: PREP **12** MINUTES; COOK **20** MINUTES

1½ cups all-purpose flour
½ teaspoon baking soda
¼ teaspoon salt
2 tablespoons sugar
1 teaspoon cream of tartar
3 tablespoons stick margarine, chilled and cut into pieces
⅔ cup sweetened dried cranberries
2 teaspoons grated orange rind
¾ cup nonfat buttermilk
1 tablespoon all-purpose flour
Vegetable cooking spray
2 teaspoons sugar

SELECTIONS

1 BREAD

1 FRUIT/VEGETABLE

1 FAT

POINTS

4

PER SERVING

186 CALORIES

32.6G CARBOHYDRATE

4.6G FAT (0.9G SATURATED)

1.2G FIBER

3.4G PROTEIN

1MG CHOLESTEROL

228MG SODIUM

34MG CALCIUM

1.3MG IRON

1. Combine first 5 ingredients in a large bowl; cut in margarine with a pastry blender until mixture resembles coarse meal. Stir in cranberries and orange rind, tossing well. Add buttermilk to dry ingredients, stirring just until dry ingredients are moistened.

2. Sprinkle 1 tablespoon flour evenly over work surface. Turn dough out onto floured surface; knead 4 or 5 times. Divide dough into 2 portions. Pat each portion into a 5-inch circle on a baking sheet coated with cooking spray. Cut each circle into 4 wedges, cutting to, but not through, bottom of dough. Sprinkle each circle evenly with 1 teaspoon sugar. Bake at 375° for 20 minutes or until golden. Yield: 8 scones (1 scone per serving).

Scones are best served right out of the oven. You can enjoy the sweet-tart taste of cranberries in this bread year-round when you use raisin-like dried cranberries.

Lemon-Blueberry Muffins

TIME: PREP 12 MINUTES; COOK 20 MINUTES

SELECTIONS

1 BREAD

POINTS

2

PER SERVING

104 CALORIES

20.9G CARBOHYDRATE

1.2G FAT (0.2G SATURATED)

0.8G FIBER

2.5G PROTEIN

0MG CHOLESTEROL

115MG SODIUM

29MG CALCIUM

0.7MG IRON

2   cups all-purpose flour
1   teaspoon baking powder
½   teaspoon baking soda
½   teaspoon salt
½   cup sugar
1   teaspoon grated lemon rind
¾   cup fresh blueberries
2   egg whites, lightly beaten
1   (8-ounce) carton lemon nonfat yogurt
½   cup unsweetened applesauce
1   tablespoon vegetable oil
Vegetable cooking spray

1. Combine first 6 ingredients in a large bowl; add blueberries, and toss to coat. Make a well in center of mixture. Combine egg whites and next 3 ingredients; add to dry ingredients, stirring just until dry ingredients are moistened.

2. Spoon batter into muffin pans coated with cooking spray, filling two-thirds full. Bake at 400° for 20 minutes. Yield: 16 muffins (1 muffin per serving).

Tangy lemon rind contrasts deliciously with sweet, fresh blueberries in these muffins. Be sure to grate only the yellow part of the rind since the white pith beneath it can be bitter.

Lemon and Dried Cherry Muffins

TIME: PREP 12 MINUTES; COOK 18 MINUTES

1¾ cups all-purpose flour
¼ cup whole wheat flour
1½ teaspoons baking powder
½ teaspoon baking soda
¼ teaspoon salt
½ cup firmly packed brown sugar
1 (3-ounce) package dried cherries
1½ cups vanilla nonfat yogurt
¼ cup fat-free egg substitute
1 tablespoon grated lemon rind
2 tablespoons fresh lemon juice
2 tablespoons stick margarine, melted
1 teaspoon vanilla extract
Vegetable cooking spray

SELECTIONS

1 BREAD

30 BONUS CALORIES

POINTS

3

PER SERVING

140 CALORIES

27.2G CARBOHYDRATE

1.8G FAT (0.3G SATURATED)

0.9G FIBER

3.4G PROTEIN

0MG CHOLESTEROL

104MG SODIUM

65MG CALCIUM

1.1MG IRON

1. Combine first 6 ingredients in a large bowl; stir well. Add cherries, and toss to coat. Make a well in center of mixture. Combine yogurt and next 5 ingredients, stirring well; add to flour mixture, stirring just until dry ingredients are moistened.

2. Spoon batter into muffin pans coated with cooking spray, filling three-fourths full. Bake at 400° for 18 minutes or until golden. Yield: 16 muffins (1 muffin per serving).

Dried cherries add a sweeter flavor than raisins to this breakfast bread, and are great for snacking, too. But if you prefer raisins, you can substitute ¾ cup raisins for the 3-ounce package of dried cherries.

Glazed Citrus Muffins *(photo, page 37)*

TIME: PREP 12 MINUTES; COOK 15 MINUTES

SELECTIONS

1 BREAD
1 FAT

POINTS

3

PER SERVING

138 CALORIES
25.9G CARBOHYDRATE
2.6G FAT (0.5G SATURATED)
0.5G FIBER
3.1G PROTEIN
1MG CHOLESTEROL
126MG SODIUM
49MG CALCIUM
1.0MG IRON

For bite-size muffins, bake this batter in miniature muffin pans at 400° for 14 minutes; then drizzle the glaze over the hot muffins while they're still in the pan. You'll get 36 muffins.

1¾	cups all-purpose flour
1	teaspoon baking powder
½	teaspoon baking soda
¼	teaspoon salt
⅓	cup sugar
¾	cup nonfat buttermilk
¼	cup fat-free egg substitute
¼	cup frozen orange juice concentrate, thawed
2	tablespoons vegetable oil
1	tablespoon grated orange rind

Vegetable cooking spray

¼	cup orange marmalade spreadable fruit
1	tablespoon fresh lemon juice
1	tablespoon water

1. Combine first 5 ingredients in a medium bowl; make a well in center of mixture. Combine buttermilk and next 4 ingredients, stirring well; add to dry ingredients, stirring just until dry ingredients are moistened.

2. Spoon batter into muffin pans coated with cooking spray, filling three-fourths full. Bake at 400° for 15 minutes. Do not remove muffins from pans.

3. Combine marmalade, lemon juice, and water in a small saucepan; place over low heat until melted, stirring often. Drizzle glaze evenly over warm muffins in pans. Remove from pans, and cool completely. Yield: 12 muffins (1 muffin per serving).

Pumpkin-Raisin Muffins

TIME: PREP 12 MINUTES; COOK 15 MINUTES

1½   cups all-purpose flour
⅓   cup firmly packed brown sugar
1   teaspoon baking powder
½   teaspoon baking soda
¼   teaspoon salt
1½   teaspoons pumpkin pie spice
⅓   cup raisins
1   egg, lightly beaten
½   cup canned pumpkin
⅓   cup orange juice
1   tablespoon stick margarine, melted
Vegetable cooking spray

1. Combine first 6 ingredients in a large bowl; stir in raisins. Make a well in center of mixture. Combine egg and next 3 ingredients in a small bowl. Add to dry ingredients, stirring just until dry ingredients are moistened. (Batter will be very thick.)

2. Spoon batter into muffin pans coated with cooking spray, filling two-thirds full. Bake at 400° for 15 minutes. Yield: 12 muffins (1 muffin per serving).

> Pumpkin pie spice is a convenient blend of spices, but you can make your own by combining ¾ teaspoon ground cinnamon, ¼ teaspoon ground ginger, and ⅛ teaspoon ground nutmeg.

SELECTIONS

1 BREAD

POINTS

2

PER SERVING

116 CALORIES

22.9G CARBOHYDRATE

1.8G FAT (0.4G SATURATED)

1.1G FIBER

2.5G PROTEIN

18MG CHOLESTEROL

122MG SODIUM

39MG CALCIUM

1.2MG IRON

Corn Muffins

TIME: PREP 8 MINUTES; COOK 20 MINUTES

2½   cups self-rising flour

3   tablespoons minced green onions

½   cup skim milk

½   cup fat-free egg substitute

1½   tablespoons vegetable oil

1   (8½-ounce) can no-salt-added cream-style corn

Vegetable cooking spray

1. Combine flour and green onions in a medium bowl; make a well in center of mixture. Combine milk and next 3 ingredients; add to dry ingredients, stirring just until dry ingredients are moistened.

2. Spoon batter into muffin pans coated with cooking spray, filling two-thirds full. Bake at 400° for 20 minutes. Remove from pans immediately, and serve warm. Yield: 12 muffins (1 muffin per serving).

Try this quick way to mince green onions: Hold several together in one hand while you snip them with kitchen shears.

Corn Sticks

TIME: PREP 9 MINUTES; COOK 10 MINUTES

¾ cup all-purpose flour
¾ cup yellow cornmeal
2 teaspoons baking powder
¼ teaspoon baking soda
¼ teaspoon salt
1½ tablespoons sugar
⅛ teaspoon ground red pepper
1 (6½-ounce) can whole-kernel corn, drained
1 egg, lightly beaten
1 cup nonfat buttermilk
Vegetable cooking spray

1. Combine first 7 ingredients in a medium bowl. Add corn, stirring well; make a well in center of mixture. Combine egg and buttermilk; add to flour mixture, stirring just until moistened.

2. Place cast-iron corn stick pans in a 425° oven for 5 minutes or until hot. Remove pans from oven, and coat with cooking spray. Spoon batter evenly into pans. Bake at 425° for 10 minutes or until lightly browned. Remove corn sticks from pans immediately, and serve warm. Yield: 14 corn sticks (1 corn stick per serving).

A preheated cast-iron pan gives cornbread a crunchy, browned crust. The batter crisps quickly in the hot pan while the inside of the bread bakes slowly and stays moist.

SELECTIONS

1 BREAD

POINTS

2

PER SERVING

83 CALORIES

16.3G CARBOHYDRATE

0.9G FAT (0.2G SATURATED)

0.7G FIBER

2.8G PROTEIN

16MG CHOLESTEROL

113MG SODIUM

51MG CALCIUM

0.8MG IRON

Strawberry Bread

TIME: PREP 10 MINUTES; COOK 1 HOUR

SELECTIONS

1 BREAD

1 FAT

POINTS

3

PER SERVING

116 CALORIES

18.8G CARBOHYDRATE

3.9G FAT (0.5G SATURATED)

0.6G FIBER

1.9G PROTEIN

0MG CHOLESTEROL

91MG SODIUM

6MG CALCIUM

0.8MG IRON

It's hard to find a good recipe for strawberry quick bread, but this one passed our taste-test with flying colors.

1½ cups all-purpose flour
½ teaspoon baking soda
¼ teaspoon salt
½ cup sugar
½ teaspoon ground cinnamon
1 egg white, lightly beaten
1 cup frozen unsweetened strawberries, thawed and coarsely chopped
2 tablespoons vegetable oil
⅓ cup chopped pecans
Vegetable cooking spray

1. Combine first 5 ingredients in a large bowl; mix well. Combine egg white, strawberries, and oil, stirring well; add to flour mixture, stirring just until dry ingredients are moistened. Stir in pecans.

2. Spoon batter into a 7½- x 3- x 2-inch loafpan coated with cooking spray. Bake at 350° for 1 hour or until a wooden pick inserted in center comes out clean. Cool in pan 10 minutes. Remove from pan, and let cool completely on a wire rack. Yield: 14 servings (1 slice per serving).

Poppy Seed Quick Bread *(photo, page 38)*

TIME: PREP 18 MINUTES; COOK 50 MINUTES

2¼ cups all-purpose flour
1 teaspoon baking powder
½ teaspoon baking soda
¼ teaspoon salt
½ cup sugar
2 tablespoons grated orange rind
1 tablespoon poppy seeds
½ cup skim milk
½ cup fresh or unsweetened orange juice
¼ cup fat-free egg substitute
2 tablespoons stick margarine, melted
½ cup chopped walnuts
Vegetable cooking spray
½ cup sifted powdered sugar
2 teaspoons fresh or unsweetened orange juice

SELECTIONS

1 BREAD

1 FAT

30 BONUS CALORIES

POINTS

3

PER SERVING

161 CALORIES

26.1G CARBOHYDRATE

5.2G FAT (0.6G SATURATED)

0.8G FIBER

3.4G PROTEIN

0MG CHOLESTEROL

103MG SODIUM

46MG CALCIUM

1.1MG IRON

1. Combine first 7 ingredients in a large bowl; mix well. Combine milk and next 3 ingredients; add to dry ingredients, stirring just until dry ingredients are moistened. Stir in walnuts.

2. Spoon batter in an 8½- x 4½- x 3-inch loafpan coated with cooking spray. Bake at 350° for 50 to 55 minutes or until a wooden pick inserted in center comes out clean.

3. Combine powdered sugar and 2 teaspoons orange juice; stir well. Drizzle glaze over hot bread in pan. Cool in pan 10 minutes. Remove from pan, and let cool completely on a wire rack. Yield: 16 servings (1 slice per serving).

You'll enjoy the flavor twist on ordinary poppy seed bread in this recipe. It has a hint of orange in the bread and a sweet orange glaze on the top.

Orange Coffee Cake with Streusel Topping

TIME: PREP 15 MINUTES; COOK 37 MINUTES

SELECTIONS

1 FAT

30 BONUS CALORIES

POINTS

3

PER SERVING

152 CALORIES

25.3G CARBOHYDRATE

4.9G FAT (0.9G SATURATED)

0.7G FIBER

2.0G PROTEIN

0MG CHOLESTEROL

110MG SODIUM

36MG CALCIUM

1.1MG IRON

2	tablespoons nutlike cereal nuggets
2	tablespoons sugar
2	teaspoons stick margarine, softened
2	egg whites, lightly beaten
¼	cup unsweetened applesauce
3	tablespoons stick margarine, melted
1	tablespoon frozen orange juice concentrate, thawed
1	(15-ounce) can mandarin oranges, drained
1	cup sifted cake flour
¼	cup sugar
1	teaspoon baking powder
⅛	teaspoon salt
¼	teaspoon ground cinnamon

Vegetable cooking spray

We used Grape-Nuts breakfast cereal to make the crunchy topping.

1. Combine first 3 ingredients in a small bowl until mixture resembles coarse meal. Set aside.

2. Combine egg whites and next 3 ingredients in a large bowl, stirring well with a wire whisk. Gently stir in oranges. Combine flour and next 4 ingredients in a medium bowl. Add flour mixture to applesauce mixture, stirring just until dry ingredients are moistened.

3. Pour batter into an 8-inch round cakepan coated with cooking spray. Sprinkle with cereal mixture. Bake at 350° for 37 minutes. Let cool in pan on a wire rack 10 minutes. Cut into wedges. Serve warm or at room temperature. Yield: 9 servings (1 wedge per serving).

Glazed Citrus Muffins
(recipe, page 30)

Poppy Seed
Quick Bread
(recipe, page 35)

Summer Fruit Crisp
(recipe, page 43)

Black Forest Parfaits
(recipe, page 52)

Lemon Cheesecake
(recipe, page 47)

desserts

Stuffed Baked Apples

TIME: PREP 7 MINUTES; COOK 40 MINUTES

SELECTIONS

1 FRUIT/VEGETABLE

1 FAT

POINTS

2

PER SERVING

115 CALORIES

23.1G CARBOHYDRATE

3.2G FAT (0.3G SATURATED)

4.5G FIBER

0.9G PROTEIN

0MG CHOLESTEROL

1MG SODIUM

25MG CALCIUM

0.5MG IRON

2   medium cooking apples

Vegetable cooking spray

1   large dried or fresh fig, finely chopped

½   teaspoon grated orange rind

¼   cup unsweetened orange juice, divided

1   tablespoon chopped pecans

¼   teaspoon ground cinnamon

1. Core apples, cutting to, but not through, bottoms; peel top third of each apple. Place apples in a 9- x 5- x 3-inch loafpan coated with cooking spray. Combine fig, orange rind, 1 tablespoon orange juice, pecans, and cinnamon in a small bowl; spoon fig mixture evenly into cavities of apples. Drizzle remaining 3 tablespoons orange juice over apples.

2. Cover and bake apples at 350° for 40 to 45 minutes or until apples are tender; baste occasionally with cooking liquid. Serve warm. Yield: 2 servings.

Any cooking apple, such as Rome, will work in this recipe, but you'll find Gala or New Zealand apples to be sweeter and crisper than most.

Summer Fruit Crisp *(photo, page 38)*

TIME: PREP 15 MINUTES; COOK 40 MINUTES

¼	cup sugar
3	tablespoons all-purpose flour
1	teaspoon grated lemon rind
3	cups sliced fresh peaches
2	cups fresh blueberries

Vegetable cooking spray

¾	cup regular oats, uncooked
⅓	cup firmly packed brown sugar
3	tablespoons whole wheat flour
2	teaspoons ground cinnamon
3	tablespoons reduced-calorie stick margarine, chilled

1. Combine first 3 ingredients in a medium bowl; stir well. Add peaches and blueberries; toss gently. Spoon mixture into an 8-inch square baking dish coated with cooking spray.

2. Combine oats and next 3 ingredients in a small bowl; cut in margarine with pastry blender until mixture is crumbly. Sprinkle over fruit mixture. Bake at 375° for 40 to 45 minutes or until topping is lightly browned. Yield: 8 servings.

> Juicy summer peaches and blueberries taste even sweeter with a cinnamon-scented topping of oats and brown sugar.

SELECTIONS

1 BREAD

2 FRUIT/VEGETABLE

1 FAT

50 BONUS CALORIES

POINTS

3

PER SERVING

209 CALORIES

46.2G CARBOHYDRATE

2.9G FAT (0.3G SATURATED)

2.6G FIBER

2.3G PROTEIN

0MG CHOLESTEROL

45MG SODIUM

130MG CALCIUM

1.2MG IRON

Strawberry-Rhubarb Crisp

TIME: PREP 10 MINUTES; COOK 40 MINUTES

SELECTIONS

1 BREAD

1 FRUIT/VEGETABLE

1 FAT

POINTS

3

PER SERVING

175 CALORIES

36.0G CARBOHYDRATE

3.5G FAT (0.5G SATURATED)

3.8G FIBER

2.6G PROTEIN

0MG CHOLESTEROL

48MG SODIUM

25MG CALCIUM

1.1MG IRON

¾   cup low-fat granola cereal without raisins

¼   cup all-purpose flour

1½   tablespoons dark brown sugar

2   tablespoons reduced-calorie stick margarine, chilled

1   cup sugar

1   tablespoon cornstarch

8   cups sliced fresh rhubarb

Vegetable cooking spray

2   cups strawberry halves

1. Combine first 4 ingredients, mixing until crumbly; set aside.

2. Combine sugar and cornstarch; set aside 3 tablespoons mixture. Combine rhubarb and remaining sugar-cornstarch mixture, tossing gently; spoon into a 13- x 9- x 2-inch baking dish coated with cooking spray. Bake, uncovered, at 325° for 25 minutes or until rhubarb is tender. Remove from oven; increase oven temperature to 375°.

3. Combine strawberries and reserved sugar-cornstarch mixture; spoon over cooked rhubarb. Sprinkle cereal mixture evenly over strawberries. Bake at 375° for 15 minutes or until bubbly. Yield: 8 servings.

The intensely tart flavor of rhubarb is traditionally paired with sweet strawberries. You can buy the reddish celery-like rhubarb stalks fresh or already cut and frozen. If you buy fresh stalks, wrap them tightly in plastic wrap, and refrigerate; they'll keep up to 3 days.

Blueberry Coffee Cake

TIME: PREP 10 MINUTES; COOK 20 MINUTES

½ cup whole grain yellow cornmeal
¼ cup plus 2 tablespoons all-purpose flour
1 teaspoon baking powder
¼ teaspoon salt
¼ cup plus 2 tablespoons sugar, divided
½ cup nonfat buttermilk
¼ cup fat-free egg substitute
1 tablespoon vegetable oil
1 teaspoon vanilla extract
Vegetable cooking spray
1½ cups fresh or frozen blueberries
½ teaspoon ground cinnamon
1 teaspoon powdered sugar

1. Combine cornmeal, flour, baking powder, salt, and ¼ cup sugar in a large bowl; make a well in center of mixture. Combine buttermilk and next 3 ingredients; add to dry ingredients, stirring just until dry ingredients are moistened. Pour batter into an 8-inch round cakepan coated with cooking spray. Top with blueberries.

2. Combine remaining 2 tablespoons sugar and cinnamon; sprinkle evenly over blueberries. Bake at 425° for 20 minutes or until a wooden pick inserted in center comes out clean. Let cool 10 minutes in pan on a wire rack; sift powdered sugar evenly over cake. Serve warm. Yield: 8 servings (1 slice per serving).

Whole grain cornmeal is sweeter than the regular kind and adds an earthy, sweet flavor to the tender cake layer. If you can't find any with "whole grain" on the label, look for stone ground, which is always whole grain.

SELECTIONS

1 BREAD

40 BONUS CALORIES

POINTS

2

PER SERVING

126 CALORIES

24.4G CARBOHYDRATE

2.2G FAT (0.4G SATURATED)

2.2G FIBER

2.7G PROTEIN

1MG CHOLESTEROL

106MG SODIUM

48MG CALCIUM

0.8MG IRON

Mexican Chocolate Cake

TIME: PREP 10 MINUTES; COOK 25 MINUTES

SELECTIONS
1 BREAD
1 FAT
30 BONUS CALORIES

POINTS
4

PER SERVING
164 CALORIES
29.0G CARBOHYDRATE
3.5G FAT (0.7G SATURATED)
0.7G FIBER
4.7G PROTEIN
1MG CHOLESTEROL
277MG SODIUM
91MG CALCIUM
1.8MG IRON

1	cup all-purpose flour
¾	teaspoon baking powder
½	teaspoon baking soda
½	teaspoon salt
½	cup firmly packed dark brown sugar
¼	cup unsweetened cocoa
½	teaspoon ground cinnamon
⅛	teaspoon ground red pepper
1	cup nonfat buttermilk
¼	cup fat-free egg substitute
1	tablespoon vegetable oil

Vegetable cooking spray

2	tablespoons finely chopped slivered almonds, toasted

1. Combine first 8 ingredients in a medium bowl; make a well in center of mixture. Combine buttermilk, egg substitute, and oil; add to dry ingredients, stirring just until dry ingredients are moistened. Pour batter into an 8-inch round cakepan coated with cooking spray. Sprinkle with almonds.

2. Bake at 375° for 25 minutes or until a wooden pick inserted in center comes out clean. Cool 10 minutes in pan on a wire rack. Serve warm. Yield: 8 servings (1 slice per serving).

The ground red pepper isn't a misprint; a pinch of it brings out a chocolate-cinnamon flavor that's traditional in Mexican chocolate desserts.

Lemon Cheesecake *(photo, page 40)*

TIME: PREP **22** MINUTES; COOK **1** HOUR; STAND **1** HOUR; CHILL **8** HOURS

1	cup finely crushed low-fat gingersnap cookie crumbs
3	tablespoons reduced-calorie margarine, melted
Vegetable cooking spray	
2	cups 1% low-fat cottage cheese
1	(8-ounce) package light process cream cheese
1	cup sugar, divided
1	cup all-purpose flour, divided
1	egg
2	egg whites
1	tablespoon plus 1 teaspoon grated lemon rind, divided
2	tablespoons fresh lemon juice, divided
1	tablespoon reduced-calorie margarine, softened

1. Combine gingersnap crumbs and 3 tablespoons margarine. Press on bottom of an 8-inch springform pan coated with cooking spray.

2. Place cottage cheese and cream cheese in container of an electric blender or food processor bowl; cover and process 1½ minutes or until smooth, stopping once to scrape down sides. Add ¾ cup sugar, ¼ cup flour, egg, egg whites, 1 tablespoon lemon rind, and 1 tablespoon lemon juice; process until blended. Pour into prepared pan. Bake at 325° for 45 minutes (center will be soft).

3. Combine remaining ¼ cup sugar, ¾ cup flour, 1 teaspoon lemon rind, 1 tablespoon lemon juice, and 1 tablespoon margarine in a small bowl, stirring until mixture resembles coarse meal. Without moving cheesecake, sprinkle flour mixture carefully over cheesecake. Bake 15 additional minutes.

4. Turn off oven; partially open oven door. Leave cheesecake in oven 1 hour. Remove from oven; let cool on a wire rack. Cover and chill 8 hours. Yield: 12 servings (1 slice per serving).

SELECTIONS

1 PROTEIN/MILK

1 FAT

150 BONUS CALORIES

POINTS

6

PER SERVING

255 CALORIES

36.9G CARBOHYDRATE

8.0G FAT (3.1G SATURATED)

0.3G FIBER

9.3G PROTEIN

31MG CHOLESTEROL

365MG SODIUM

54MG CALCIUM

0.8MG IRON

You won't believe this cheesecake is low fat when you taste the creamy texture. Add a garnish of lemon slices and mint sprigs to dress it up, if you wish.

Pumpkin Cheesecake

TIME: PREP 10 MINUTES; COOK 50 MINUTES; STAND 1 HOUR; CHILL 8 HOURS

SELECTIONS
1 PROTEIN/MILK
1 BREAD

POINTS
4

PER SERVING
196 CALORIES
31.6G CARBOHYDRATE
0.9G FAT (0.4G SATURATED)
1.0G FIBER
15.8G PROTEIN
7MG CHOLESTEROL
300MG SODIUM
312MG CALCIUM
1.1MG IRON

¾ cup finely crushed reduced-fat honey graham cracker crumbs (about 12 cracker squares)

Vegetable cooking spray

¾ cup nonfat ricotta cheese

¾ cup fat-free egg substitute

⅔ cup 1% low-fat cottage cheese

½ cup canned pumpkin

1⅓ cups instant nonfat dry milk powder

⅓ cup sugar

1 tablespoon all-purpose flour

½ teaspoon ground cinnamon

1 tablespoon lemon juice

1 teaspoon vanilla extract

1. Sprinkle graham cracker crumbs evenly in bottom of an 8-inch springform pan coated with cooking spray. Set aside.

2. Place ricotta cheese and remaining 9 ingredients in container of an electric blender or food processor bowl. Cover and process until smooth, stopping once to scrape down sides. Pour cheese mixture over crumbs in springform pan.

3. Bake at 300° for 50 minutes or until center is almost set (center will be soft but will firm when chilled). Turn off oven; partially open oven door. Leave cheesecake in oven 1 hour. Remove from oven; let cool on a wire rack. Cover and chill 8 hours. Yield: 8 servings (1 slice per serving).

We've never seen an easier cheese-cake recipe—only 10 minutes preparation. And, with less than 1 gram of fat per slice, it's the perfect guilt-free dessert for the Thanksgiving holidays.

Key Lime Pie

TIME: PREP **8** MINUTES; COOK **10** MINUTES; CHILL **2** HOURS

1¼   cups finely crushed low-fat chocolate graham cracker crumbs
        (about 9 cracker squares)
¼   cup reduced-calorie margarine, melted
1   (14-ounce) can nonfat sweetened condensed milk
½   cup fresh Key lime or lime juice
1   tablespoon grated Key lime or lime rind
1½   cups frozen reduced-calorie whipped topping,
        thawed and divided
8 thin slices Key lime or lime

SELECTIONS

1 PROTEIN/MILK

1 FAT

130 BONUS CALORIES

POINTS

5

PER SERVING

233 CALORIES

13.6G CARBOHYDRATE

6.1G FAT (0.6G SATURATED)

0.1G FIBER

2.3G PROTEIN

3MG CHOLESTEROL

165MG SODIUM

111MG CALCIUM

0.3MG IRON

1. Combine graham cracker crumbs and margarine; stir well. Press in bottom and up sides of a 9-inch pieplate. Bake at 350° for 10 minutes. Remove from oven; let cool on a wire rack.

2. Combine milk and lime juice in a bowl; stir until blended. Stir in lime rind; gently fold in ¾ cup whipped topping. Pour into prepared crust. Cover and chill at least 2 hours. Top each slice with 1½ tablespoons whipped topping and a lime slice. Yield: 8 servings (1 slice per serving).

Key limes are smaller and more yellow-skinned than regular limes, and the flavor of Key limes is not as acidic. Look for them in specialty produce sections of the supermarket. If you can't find them, substitute regular limes. Fresh juice will taste better than the bottled type.

Chocolate Mousse

TIME: PREP 9 MINUTES; CHILL 2 HOURS

SELECTIONS
120 BONUS CALORIES

POINTS
3

PER SERVING
127 CALORIES
18.9G CARBOHYDRATE
4.4G FAT (1.5G SATURATED)
0.0G FIBER
3.0G PROTEIN
1MG CHOLESTEROL
36MG SODIUM
27MG CALCIUM
0.7MG IRON

1   envelope unflavored gelatin
1   cup cold water
2   tablespoons unsweetened cocoa
¼   cup plus 2 tablespoons chocolate syrup
2¾   cups frozen reduced-calorie whipped topping,
      thawed and divided

1. Sprinkle gelatin over cold water in a small saucepan; let stand 1 minute. Cook over low heat, stirring constantly, about 2 minutes or until gelatin dissolves. Remove from heat; let cool.

2. Add cocoa and chocolate syrup to gelatin mixture, stirring with a wire whisk until smooth. Fold in 2 cups whipped topping. Spoon evenly into 6 individual dessert dishes. Cover and chill 2 hours or until firm. Before serving, top each serving with 2 tablespoons whipped topping. Yield: 6 servings (½ cup per serving).

With just 5 ingredients and in less than 10 minutes, you can put this chocolatey dessert in the fridge for later. It was a favorite with our staff.

Crème Caramel

TIME: PREP 13 MINUTES; COOK 30 MINUTES; CHILL 2 HOURS

½	cup sugar, divided
1	(12-ounce) can evaporated skimmed milk
½	cup fat-free egg substitute
½	teaspoon grated orange rind
1	teaspoon vanilla extract
¼	teaspoon almond extract

SELECTIONS

1 PROTEIN/MILK

110 BONUS CALORIES

POINTS

4

PER SERVING

182 CALORIES

35.3G CARBOHYDRATE

0.2G FAT (0.1G SATURATED)

0.0G FIBER

9.4G PROTEIN

3MG CHOLESTEROL

143MG SODIUM

257MG CALCIUM

0.8MG IRON

1. Place ¼ cup plus 2 tablespoons sugar in a cast-iron or heavy skillet. Cook over medium heat, stirring constantly, until sugar melts and turns light brown. Pour melted sugar into 4 (6-ounce) custard cups, tilting to coat bottoms; place in an 8- or 9-inch square pan. Set aside.

2. Pour milk in a small saucepan. Cook over medium heat until thoroughly heated (do not boil). Set aside.

3. Combine remaining 2 tablespoons sugar, egg substitute, orange rind, and flavorings, stirring well. Gradually stir about one-fourth of hot milk into egg substitute mixture; add to remaining hot mixture, stirring constantly.

4. Pour milk mixture evenly into prepared custard cups; pour hot water into pan to depth of 1 inch. Bake at 350° for 30 minutes or until a knife inserted in center comes out clean. Remove custard cups from water, and let cool on a wire rack.

5. Cover and chill at least 2 hours. Loosen edges of custards with a knife; invert onto individual serving plates. Yield: 4 servings.

Cast iron is best for caramelizing sugar because it heats slowly. That's the key to caramelized, not burnt, sugar for a gooey sugar topping. You also can use a heavy skillet.

Black Forest Parfaits *(photo, page 39)*

TIME: PREP 8 MINUTES

SELECTIONS

140 BONUS CALORIES

POINTS

4

PER SERVING

195 CALORIES

41.3G CARBOHYDRATE

1.8G FAT (0.4G SATURATED)

0.8G FIBER

4.3G PROTEIN

2MG CHOLESTEROL

335MG SODIUM

127MG CALCIUM

0.6MG IRON

1   (3.4-ounce) package fat-free white chocolate instant
       pudding mix
2   cups skim milk
1   (20-ounce) can light cherry pie filling
¾   cup chocolate wafer cookie crumbs (about 16 cookies)
¼   cup plus 2 tablespoons frozen reduced-calorie
       whipped topping, thawed
Fresh cherries (optional)

1. Prepare pudding mix according to package directions, using
skim milk.

2. Divide half of pudding evenly among 6 (6-ounce) parfait or
stemmed glasses. Spoon half of pie filling evenly over pudding in
glasses. Top parfaits evenly with half of cookie crumbs. Repeat layers
with remaining pudding, pie filling, and cookie crumbs. Top each
serving with 1 tablespoon whipped topping, and garnish with fresh
cherries, if desired. Yield: 6 servings.

> Layers of rich white chocolate pudding and sweet cherries
> make this dessert look special enough for company, yet it's quick
> enough to make on the spur-of-the-moment for family. You can serve
> the parfaits right after you make them, but it's okay to chill them for
> later, too.

Raspberry-Orange Yogurt

TIME: PREP 7 MINUTES; FREEZE 8 HOURS

2   (10-ounce) packages frozen raspberries in light syrup, thawed
½   teaspoon grated orange rind
½   cup unsweetened orange juice
1   (8-ounce) carton raspberry nonfat yogurt

1. Position knife blade in food processor bowl; add raspberries. Process until smooth. Pour puree into a wire-mesh strainer; press with back of a spoon against the sides of strainer to squeeze out juice. Discard seeds remaining in strainer. Combine strained puree, orange rind, orange juice, and yogurt, stirring well with a wire whisk. Pour mixture into an 8-inch square pan. Cover and freeze 8 hours or until firm.

2. Position knife blade in food processor; add frozen raspberry mixture. Process until smooth, but not thawed. To serve, scoop into 8 individual dessert dishes. Serve immediately. Yield: 4 cups (½ cup per serving).

SELECTIONS

1 FRUIT/VEGETABLE

60 BONUS CALORIES

POINTS

1

PER SERVING

99 CALORIES

23.9G CARBOHYDRATE

0.1G FAT (0.0G SATURATED)

5.0G FIBER

1.6G PROTEIN

0MG CHOLESTEROL

17MG SODIUM

42MG CALCIUM

0.5MG IRON

If you like a puckery citrus flavor in desserts, you'll love this one. Orange rind adds to the fresh flavor; just grate the rind before you extract juice from the orange for easier grating.

Strawberry Whip

SELECTIONS

1 BREAD

1 FRUIT/VEGETABLE

1 FAT

40 BONUS CALORIES

POINTS

1

PER SERVING

57 CALORIES

12.0G CARBOHYDRATE

0.9G FAT (0.4G SATURATED)

0.6G FIBER

0.2G PROTEIN

0MG CHOLESTEROL

5MG SODIUM

5MG CALCIUM

0.3MG IRON

3   (10-ounce) packages frozen strawberries in light syrup,
        partially thawed
2   tablespoons fresh lime juice
1   cup reduced-calorie frozen whipped topping, thawed

1. Position knife blade in food processor bowl; add strawberries and lime juice. Process until smooth, stopping once to scrape down sides. Fold in whipped topping; serve immediately. Yield: 5 cups (½ cup per serving).

To partially thaw strawberries, place all 3 packages in a large bowl, cover them with hot water, and let stand for 5 minutes.

Fudgy Brownies

TIME: PREP **6** MINUTES; COOK **25** MINUTES

½   cup unsweetened cocoa
½   cup sugar
⅓   cup all-purpose flour
½   teaspoon baking powder
½   teaspoon salt
½   cup apple butter
½   cup fat-free egg substitute
2   tablespoons vegetable oil
1   teaspoon vanilla extract
Vegetable cooking spray
2   tablespoons chopped walnuts

1. Combine first 5 ingredients in a medium bowl, stirring well. Combine apple butter and next 3 ingredients in a large bowl. Gradually add cocoa mixture to apple butter mixture, stirring with a wire whisk.

2. Pour batter into an 8-inch square pan coated with cooking spray; sprinkle evenly with chopped walnuts. Bake at 350° for 25 minutes or until a wooden pick inserted in center comes out clean. Let cool completely on a wire rack. Cut into 16 squares. Yield: 16 brownies (1 per serving).

SELECTIONS

1 FAT

30 BONUS CALORIES

POINTS

2

PER SERVING

90 CALORIES

14.1G CARBOHYDRATE

2.9G FAT (0.6G SATURATED)

0.2G FIBER

2.1G PROTEIN

0MG CHOLESTEROL

86MG SODIUM

17MG CALCIUM

0.8MG IRON

Apple butter replaces some of the fat and keeps the brownies fudgy and moist. One bite and you'll never believe they're less than 3 grams of fat each.

Raisin-Bran Cookies

TIME: PREP 16 MINUTES; COOK 10 MINUTES

¼ cup margarine, softened
⅓ cup sugar
2 tablespoons honey
¼ cup fat-free egg substitute
1 teaspoon vanilla extract
1 cup regular oats, uncooked
¾ cup all-purpose flour
½ teaspoon baking powder
¼ teaspoon baking soda
¼ teaspoon salt
⅓ cup instant nonfat dry milk powder
¾ cup raisins
1¼ cups wheat bran flakes cereal
Vegetable cooking spray

1. Beat margarine, sugar, and honey in a large mixing bowl at medium-high speed of an electric mixer until creamy. Add egg substitute and vanilla, beating well.

2. Combine oats and next 5 ingredients; gradually add to creamed mixture, beating well. Stir in raisins and bran flakes.

3. Drop dough by rounded tablespoonfuls onto baking sheets coated with cooking spray. Bake at 350° for 10 minutes or until golden. Transfer to wire racks, and let cool completely. Yield: 24 cookies (1 per serving).

Savor a warm oatmeal cookie right from the oven with a glass of skim milk when you need a sweet snack. Honey adds extra flavor and helps the cookies to stay soft and moist.

Oven-Fried Catfish
(recipe, page 61)

Grouper à la Mango
(recipe, page 64)

fish
shellfish

Lime-Marinated Grilled Sea Bass *(photo, page 1)*

SELECTIONS

1 PROTEIN/MILK

1 FAT

POINTS

3

PER SERVING

138 CALORIES

1.4G CARBOHYDRATE

4.7G FAT (0.9G SATURATED)

0.1G FIBER

21.0G PROTEIN

47MG CHOLESTEROL

177MG SODIUM

16MG CALCIUM

0.5MG IRON

¼ cup dry vermouth or dry white wine

2 tablespoons fresh lime juice

2 tablespoons minced fresh cilantro

1 tablespoon low-sodium soy sauce

2 teaspoons olive oil

4 (4-ounce) sea bass fillets (1 inch thick)

Vegetable cooking spray

1. Combine first 5 ingredients in a heavy-duty, zip-top plastic bag; add fish fillets. Seal bag securely, and shake gently to coat fillets. Marinate in refrigerator 30 minutes.

2. Coat grill rack with cooking spray; place on grill over hot coals (400° to 500°). Remove fish from marinade, reserving marinade. Place fish fillets on rack; grill, covered, 4 to 5 minutes on each side or until fish flakes easily when tested with a fork.

3. Place reserved marinade in a small saucepan, and bring to a boil; remove from heat. To serve, spoon marinade mixture over fish. Yield: 4 servings.

> If you can't find sea bass, substitute grouper; they're from the same family. Grouper fillets aren't as thick though, so you'll need to cut the grilling time in half.

Oven-Fried Catfish *(photo, page 57)*

TIME: PREP 14 MINUTES; COOK 18 MINUTES

1   cup plus 2 tablespoons crushed corn flakes cereal
1½   teaspoons salt-free Creole seasoning
¼   teaspoon salt
¼   cup nonfat mayonnaise
1   tablespoon lemon juice
½   teaspoon hot sauce
8   (4-ounce) farm-raised catfish fillets
Vegetable cooking spray
8   lemon wedges

1. Combine first 3 ingredients in a small bowl, stirring well; set aside. Combine mayonnaise, lemon juice, and hot sauce, stirring well.

2. Brush mayonnaise mixture evenly over both sides of fillets; dredge in cereal mixture. Place fillets on rack of a broiler pan coated with cooking spray. Bake at 450° for 18 minutes or until fish flakes easily when tested with a fork. Serve with lemon wedges. Yield: 8 servings.

> The crispy oven-fried crust comes from baking the crumb-coated fillets at a high temperature. Creole seasoning gives the crunchy crust its great flavor.

SELECTIONS

1 PROTEIN/MILK

1 BREAD

POINTS

5

PER SERVING

205 CALORIES

17.0G CARBOHYDRATE

4.9G FAT (1.1G SATURATED)

0.2G FIBER

21.9G PROTEIN

66MG CHOLESTEROL

403MG SODIUM

51MG CALCIUM

2.1MG IRON

Easy Parmesan Flounder

TIME: PREP 5 MINUTES; COOK 6 MINUTES

SELECTIONS

2 PROTEIN/MILK

1 FAT

POINTS

4

PER SERVING

153 CALORIES

3.6G CARBOHYDRATE

4.8G FAT (1.3G SATURATED)

0.0G FIBER

22.7G PROTEIN

62MG CHOLESTEROL

403MG SODIUM

103MG CALCIUM

0.4MG IRON

4	(4-ounce) flounder fillets
	Vegetable cooking spray
1	tablespoon lemon juice
¼	cup nonfat mayonnaise
3	tablespoons grated Parmesan cheese
1	tablespoon thinly sliced green onions
1	tablespoon reduced-calorie margarine, softened
⅛	teaspoon hot sauce

1. Place fillets on rack of a broiler pan coated with cooking spray; brush fillets with lemon juice. Broil 5½ inches from heat (with electric oven door partially opened) 5 to 6 minutes or until fish flakes easily when tested with a fork.

2. Combine mayonnaise and remaining 4 ingredients, stirring well. Spread mayonnaise mixture evenly over 1 side of fillets. Broil 1 additional minute or until lightly browned and bubbly. Yield: 4 servings.

A simple mayonnaise-Parmesan topping turns these flounder fillets into a special dinner—in less than 15 minutes.

Grouper à la Mango *(photo, page 58)*

TIME: PREP 13 MINUTES; COOK 20 MINUTES

1½   cups finely chopped fresh mango (about 2 mangoes)
½   cup finely chopped sweet red pepper
⅓   cup finely chopped purple onion
¼   cup chopped fresh cilantro
2   tablespoons fresh lime juice
½   teaspoon salt, divided
4   (4-ounce) grouper fillets
¼   teaspoon ground red pepper
Vegetable cooking spray
Fresh cilantro sprigs (optional)

1. Combine mango, sweet red pepper, onion, chopped cilantro, lime juice, and ¼ teaspoon salt in a small bowl; toss well to combine. Set aside or chill, if desired.

2. Sprinkle fillets evenly with remaining ¼ teaspoon salt and ground red pepper; arrange in an 11- x 7- x 1½-inch baking dish coated with cooking spray. Bake at 425° for 20 minutes or until fish flakes easily when tested with a fork. Serve with mango salsa. Garnish with cilantro sprigs, if desired. Yield: 4 servings (1 fillet and ½ cup salsa per serving).

> Mango, sweet red pepper, onion, cilantro, and lime juice make a colorful, tropical-tasting salsa that's good served with fish or grilled chicken. Serve the salsa at room temperature or chilled.

SELECTIONS

1 PROTEIN/MILK

1 FRUIT/VEGETABLE

40 BONUS CALORIES

POINTS

3

PER SERVING

159 CALORIES

13.5G CARBOHYDRATE

1.6G FAT (0.3G SATURATED)

1.6G FIBER

22.7G PROTEIN

42MG CHOLESTEROL

343MG SODIUM

32MG CALCIUM

1.5MG IRON

Grilled Mahimahi with Tomato Vinaigrette

TIME: PREP 10 MINUTES; COOK 8 MINUTES

SELECTIONS

1 PROTEIN/MILK
1 FRUIT/VEGETABLE
1 FAT

POINTS

3

PER SERVING

139 CALORIES
4.7G CARBOHYDRATE
3.5G FAT (0.6G SATURATED)
1.2G FIBER
21.8G PROTEIN
83MG CHOLESTEROL
220MG SODIUM
5MG CALCIUM
1.8MG IRON

6   medium tomatoes, sliced
Olive oil-flavored vegetable cooking spray
2   tablespoons balsamic vinegar
1   tablespoon olive oil
½   teaspoon sugar
¼   teaspoon ground pepper
1   tablespoon capers, drained
6   (4-ounce) mahimahi fillets (½ inch thick)

1. Arrange tomato slices on a large baking sheet. Coat slices with cooking spray, and broil 3 inches from heat (with electric oven door partially opened) 6 to 8 minutes or until browned.

2. Position knife blade in food processor bowl; add tomato, vinegar, and next 3 ingredients. Process until smooth, stopping once to scrape down sides. Add capers, and set aside.

3. Coat grill rack with cooking spray. Place on grill over medium-hot coals (350° to 400°). Place fillets on rack; grill, covered, 4 to 5 minutes on each side or until fish flakes easily when tested with a fork. Transfer fillets to a serving platter; top evenly with vinaigrette. Yield: 6 servings (1 fillet and ¼ cup vinaigrette per serving).

A tangy-sweet tomato vinaigrette drapes these grilled fish fillets with extra flavor, and tastes just as good served over other firm, white fish fillets. You can use red wine vinegar instead of balsamic, but balsamic vinegar has a distinctive mellow flavor that makes it worth keeping on your pantry shelf.

Sesame Salmon

TIME: PREP 4 MINUTES; COOK 8 MINUTES

1   tablespoon reduced-sodium soy sauce
1   teaspoon sesame oil
4   (4-ounce) salmon fillets
1½   teaspoons sesame seeds
Vegetable cooking spray

1. Combine soy sauce and sesame oil. Brush mixture evenly over salmon fillets. Sprinkle sesame seeds over 1 side of fillets.

2. Coat a large nonstick skillet with cooking spray, and place over medium-high heat. Add salmon; cook 4 minutes on each side or until fish flakes easily when tested with a fork. Yield: 4 servings.

Salmon is naturally high in fat and has a strong, rich flavor. So it needs only a few simple seasonings such as soy sauce and sesame oil and seeds to dress it up. Sesame oil is strong-flavored, so you need only a small amount to make a flavor impact.

SELECTIONS

3 PROTEIN/MILK

POINTS

5

PER SERVING

210 CALORIES

0.3G CARBOHYDRATE

11.5G FAT (1.9G SATURATED)

0.1G FIBER

24.4G PROTEIN

77MG CHOLESTEROL

156MG SODIUM

18MG CALCIUM

0.7MG IRON

Cheese-Stuffed Swordfish

TIME: PREP 20 MINUTES; COOK 10 MINUTES

SELECTIONS

2 PROTEIN/MILK

40 BONUS CALORIES

POINTS

5

PER SERVING

205 CALORIES

3.4G CARBOHYDRATE

8.1G FAT (3.3G SATURATED)

0.3G FIBER

27.8G PROTEIN

55MG CHOLESTEROL

424MG SODIUM

151MG CALCIUM

1.3MG IRON

3	tablespoons grated Parmesan cheese
2	tablespoons fine, dry breadcrumbs
1	tablespoon drained capers, minced
1	tablespoon minced fresh parsley
½	teaspoon ground pepper
1	clove garlic, minced
1	(1-pound) swordfish fillet (about 2 inches thick)
2	ounces part-skim mozzarella cheese, cut into 4 equal slices

Olive oil-flavored vegetable cooking spray

1. Combine first 6 ingredients; mix well. Set aside.

2. Cut swordfish fillet into 4 equal pieces; cut a pocket in each piece, cutting to, but not through, remaining 3 sides. Place cheese slices in fish pockets; secure openings with wooden picks. Coat fillets with cooking spray; dredge in crumb mixture.

3. Coat grill rack with cooking spray; place on grill over medium-hot coals (350° to 400°). Place fish on rack; grill, covered, 5 minutes on each side or until fish flakes easily when tested with a fork. Serve immediately. Yield: 4 servings.

These steaklike swordfish fillets are stuffed with mozzarella cheese and coated with a garlic, parsley, and caper crumb mixture before they're grilled to perfection—all in 30 minutes. If you're cooking for guests, stuff the fish before company arrives, and keep the prepared fish in the refrigerator. Then coat the fish with the crumb mixture and grill it for 10 minutes before dinnertime.

Herb-Baked Trout

TIME: PREP 8 MINUTES; COOK 13 MINUTES

¼   cup minced fresh basil
¼   cup fresh lemon juice
2   teaspoons olive oil
4   (4-ounce) rainbow trout fillets
Vegetable cooking spray
½   teaspoon ground pepper
¼   teaspoon salt
1   small lemon, thinly sliced

1. Combine first 3 ingredients in a liquid measuring cup; set aside.

2. Place trout in a 13- x 9- x 2-inch baking dish coated with cooking spray. Sprinkle fillets with pepper and salt; top with lemon slices. Pour half of basil mixture over trout. Bake at 350° for 13 to 15 minutes or until fish flakes easily when tested with a fork. Spoon remaining basil mixture over fish, and serve immediately. Yield: 4 servings.

Substitute ¼ cup of your favorite fresh herb for basil in this dish. To mince leafy herbs quickly, pack the herbs in a measuring cup, and use kitchen shears.

SELECTIONS

1 PROTEIN/MILK

50 BONUS CALORIES

POINTS

4

PER SERVING

155 CALORIES

1.3G CARBOHYDRATE

5.8G FAT (1.0G SATURATED)

0.1G FIBER

23.5G PROTEIN

65MG CHOLESTEROL

177MG SODIUM

82MG CALCIUM

2.2MG IRON

Crab Cakes *(photo, page 76)*

TIME: PREP 15 MINUTES; COOK 12 MINUTES

SELECTIONS

2 PROTEIN/MILK

1 BREAD

1 FAT

POINTS

5

PER SERVING

217 CALORIES

13.3G CARBOHYDRATE

7.0G FAT (1.1G SATURATED)

0.7G FIBER

23.9G PROTEIN

102MG CHOLESTEROL

547MG SODIUM

128MG CALCIUM

1.7MG IRON

1	pound fresh lump crabmeat, drained
1½	cups soft breadcrumbs
¼	cup chopped green onions
2	tablespoons reduced-calorie mayonnaise
1½	tablespoons lemon juice
1	tablespoon chopped fresh parsley
1½	teaspoons Dijon mustard
1½	teaspoons Worcestershire sauce
1	teaspoon ground pepper
¼	teaspoon hot sauce
2	egg whites, lightly beaten

Vegetable cooking spray

2 teaspoons vegetable oil, divided

Fat-free tartar sauce or Radish Tartar Sauce (optional)

Lemon wedges (optional)

1. Combine first 11 ingredients in a medium bowl, stirring well. Shape mixture into 8 (½-inch-thick) patties.

2. Coat a large nonstick skillet with cooking spray; add 1 teaspoon oil, and place over medium heat until hot. Place 4 patties in skillet, and cook 3 minutes on each side or until golden. Repeat procedure with remaining 1 teaspoon oil and 4 patties. Place 2 crab cakes on each individual serving plate; top each crab cake with 1 tablespoon fat-free tartar sauce or Radish Tartar Sauce, if desired. Garnish with lemon wedges, if desired. Yield: 4 servings (2 crab cakes per serving).

Most of the preparation time is spent picking through the crabmeat to remove bits of cartilage from the flakes of crab. It's tedious, but well worth the effort.

Radish Tartar Sauce *(photo, page 76)*

TIME: PREP 8 MINUTES; CHILL 1 HOUR

¾	cup finely chopped radish
½	cup nonfat sour cream
⅓	cup minced green onions
¼	cup reduced-calorie mayonnaise
1	tablespoon capers, drained
1	tablespoon prepared horseradish
⅛	teaspoon salt

SELECTIONS

FREE

POINTS

0

PER SERVING

11 CALORIES

0.8G CARBOHYDRATE

0.7G FAT (0.1G SATURATED)

0.1G FIBER

0.4G PROTEIN

1MG CHOLESTEROL

62MG SODIUM

8MG CALCIUM

0.0MG IRON

1. Combine all ingredients; stir well. Cover and chill at least 1 hour. Serve with crab cakes or fish. Stir well before serving. Yield: 1½ cups (2 tablespoons per serving).

The bite in this Radish Tartar Sauce was so refreshing with the Crab Cakes on page 68 that we suggest taking 8 minutes to whip it up whenever you serve Crab Cakes. Serve the leftover sauce with any type of fish.

Shrimp Fried Rice

TIME: PREP 7 MINUTES; COOK 15 MINUTES

SELECTIONS

1 PROTEIN/MILK

1 BREAD

POINTS

4

PER SERVING

206 CALORIES

27.4G CARBOHYDRATE

3.6G FAT (0.8G SATURATED)

3.1G FIBER

15.0G PROTEIN

96MG CHOLESTEROL

302MG SODIUM

53MG CALCIUM

2.1MG IRON

Make the brown rice in advance, and chill it if you don't want it to clump together like traditional "sticky" rice.

1 pound unpeeled medium size fresh shrimp
1 egg, lightly beaten
3 egg whites, lightly beaten
Vegetable cooking spray
2 teaspoons vegetable oil
1 cup finely chopped green onions
½ cup finely chopped carrot
½ cup finely chopped celery
1 clove garlic, minced
1 cup frozen English peas, thawed
4 cups cooked brown rice (cooked without salt or fat)
2 tablespoons reduced-sodium soy sauce
¼ teaspoon salt

1. Peel and devein shrimp; coarsely chop, and set aside.

2. Combine egg and egg whites; set aside.

3. Coat a wok or large nonstick skillet with cooking spray; drizzle oil around top of wok, coating sides. Heat at medium-high (375°) until hot. Add shrimp; stir-fry 2 to 3 minutes or until shrimp turn pink. Remove from wok, and set aside.

4. Add green onions and next 3 ingredients to wok; stir-fry 3 minutes or until crisp-tender. Add egg mixture, stirring gently until set. Add peas, and stir-fry 2 minutes. Add rice, and stir-fry 2 minutes. Add cooked shrimp, soy sauce, and salt, and stir-fry until thoroughly heated. Serve immediately. Yield: 8 servings (1 cup per serving).

meatless
main dishes

Eggs Sardou

TIME: PREP 20 MINUTES; COOK 20 MINUTES

SELECTIONS

2 PROTEIN/MILK

2 FRUIT/VEGETABLE

POINTS

5

PER SERVING

220 CALORIES

18.7G CARBOHYDRATE

9.2G FAT (3.0G SATURATED)

3.3G FIBER

17.3G PROTEIN

219MG CHOLESTEROL

556MG SODIUM

366MG CALCIUM

3.2MG IRON

Vegetable cooking spray

½   cup chopped green onions

1   (9-ounce) package frozen artichoke hearts, thawed

8   cups tightly packed torn fresh spinach

¼   cup water

4   hard-cooked eggs, peeled and sliced

1   cup evaporated skimmed milk

1½ tablespoons all-purpose flour

¼   cup grated Parmesan cheese, divided

2   tablespoons fresh lemon juice

2   teaspoons reduced-calorie margarine

2   teaspoons Dijon mustard

¼   teaspoon salt

¼   teaspoon ground pepper

If you don't have individual gratin dishes, make a single casserole in a shallow 1-quart casserole dish.

1. Coat a large nonstick skillet with cooking spray. Place over medium-high heat until hot. Add green onions and artichokes, and cook 2 minutes or until tender, stirring often. Add spinach and water to skillet; stir lightly to mix. Cover and cook 4 minutes or until spinach wilts. Uncover and cook 3 minutes or until liquid evaporates. Spoon mixture into 4 (1-cup) gratin dishes coated with cooking spray. Arrange egg slices evenly over spinach mixture; set aside.

2. Combine milk and flour in a small saucepan; stir until smooth. Cook over medium heat, stirring constantly, until thickened. Remove from heat; stir in 2 tablespoons Parmesan cheese and remaining 5 ingredients.

3. Pour cheese sauce evenly over egg in gratin dishes. Sprinkle with remaining 2 tablespoons Parmesan cheese. Cover and bake at 350° for 20 minutes. Yield: 4 servings.

Zesty Breakfast Burritos *(photo, page 77)*

TIME: PREP 15 MINUTES; COOK 7 MINUTES

3	eggs
6	egg whites
¼	teaspoon salt
½	teaspoon chili powder
¼	teaspoon ground red pepper
1	(4½-ounce) can chopped green chiles, drained
½	cup chopped roasted red pepper
1	teaspoon reduced-calorie margarine
8	(8-inch) flour tortillas
½	cup (2 ounces) shredded reduced-fat Cheddar cheese
¾	cup salsa
¼	cup plus 2 tablespoons nonfat sour cream

Fresh cilantro sprigs (optional)

1. Combine first 5 ingredients in a medium bowl; stir well. Add green chiles and red pepper.

2. Melt margarine in a large nonstick skillet over medium heat. Add egg mixture, and cook until mixture is firm, but still moist, stirring often.

3. Spoon egg mixture evenly down center of each tortilla; top evenly with cheese. Roll up tortillas; place on a serving plate, seam side down. Top each burrito evenly with salsa and sour cream. Garnish with cilantro sprigs, if desired. Yield: 8 servings (1 burrito per serving).

SELECTIONS

1 PROTEIN/MILK

1 BREAD

POINTS

5

PER SERVING

220 CALORIES

28.1G CARBOHYDRATE

6.5G FAT (1.9G SATURATED)

1.6G FIBER

11.5G PROTEIN

87MG CHOLESTEROL

584MG SODIUM

123MG CALCIUM

1.7MG IRON

To roast your own peppers, broil flattened pepper halves 15 minutes or until the skins are black. Then plunge them into ice water; peel and discard the skins.

Vegetable-Bean Hot Pot *(photo, opposite page)*

TIME: PREP 8 MINUTES; COOK 35 MINUTES

SELECTIONS

1 BREAD

1 FRUIT/VEGETABLE

POINTS

3

PER SERVING

198 CALORIES

35.4G CARBOHYDRATE

2.1G FAT (1.0G SATURATED)

6.0G FIBER

11.8G PROTEIN

4MG CHOLESTEROL

578MG SODIUM

138MG CALCIUM

4.3MG IRON

It's easier (and safer for your fingers) to slice mushrooms with an egg slicer.

Vegetable cooking spray
1   cup chopped carrot
½   cup chopped onion
1   cup chopped sweet red pepper
1   (14½-ounce) can no-salt-added stewed tomatoes, undrained
1   cup water
2   tablespoons tomato paste
1   teaspoon onion powder
1   teaspoon garlic powder
½   teaspoon salt
½   teaspoon ground cumin
1   (16-ounce) can red kidney beans, drained
½   cup sliced fresh mushrooms
2   tablespoons plus 2 teaspoons freshly grated Parmesan cheese
2   tablespoons plus 2 teaspoons chopped fresh parsley

1. Coat a large saucepan with cooking spray; place over medium-high heat until hot. Add carrot and onion; cook, stirring constantly, 3 minutes or until onion is soft. Add red pepper, and cook, stirring constantly, 1 minute.

2. Stir in tomato and next 6 ingredients; bring to a boil. Cover, reduce heat, and simmer 30 minutes or until carrot is tender. Stir in kidney beans and mushrooms; cook, uncovered, 5 additional minutes. Ladle into individual serving bowls; sprinkle each serving with 2 teaspoons each of Parmesan cheese and parsley. Yield: 4 servings.

Crab Cakes (*recipe, page 68*);
Radish Tartar Sauce (*recipe, page 69*)

Zesty Breakfast Burritos
(*recipe, page 73*)

Ratatouille Rigatoni
(*recipe, page 85*)

Vegetable Pizza *(photo, opposite page)*

TIME: PREP 20 MINUTES; COOK 17 MINUTES

Vegetable cooking spray

1	tablespoon cornmeal
1	(10-ounce) can refrigerated pizza dough
1	medium-size purple onion, thinly sliced
2	cloves garlic, very thinly sliced
1	teaspoon olive oil
¼	pound fresh green beans
1	cup (4 ounces) shredded part-skim mozzarella cheese
½	cup nonfat ricotta cheese
¼	cup minced fresh basil
½	teaspoon ground pepper
3	tablespoons sliced ripe olives
4	plum tomatoes, thinly sliced
¼	cup freshly grated Parmesan cheese

SELECTIONS

1 PROTEIN/MILK

2 BREAD

1 FRUIT/VEGETABLE

POINTS

5

PER SERVING

252 CALORIES

33.8G CARBOHYDRATE

7.4G FAT (3.0G SATURATED)

3.0G FIBER

14.3G PROTEIN

15MG CHOLESTEROL

470MG SODIUM

224MG CALCIUM

1.2MG IRON

1. Coat a 15- x 10- x 1-inch jellyroll pan with cooking spray; sprinkle with cornmeal. Unroll pizza dough; press into pan.

2. Coat a large nonstick skillet with cooking spray; place over medium-high heat until hot. Add onion, and cook 6 minutes or until tender, stirring often. Add garlic, and cook 2 minutes, stirring often. Remove from skillet, and set aside.

3. Add olive oil to skillet; place over medium-high heat until hot. Add green beans, and cook 2 minutes, stirring often. Set aside.

4. Combine mozzarella cheese and next 3 ingredients; stir well. Spread mixture evenly over pizza crust, leaving a ½-inch border. Arrange onion, garlic, and beans over cheese mixture; top with olives and tomato. Sprinkle with Parmesan cheese. Bake at 450° for 12 minutes or until crust is browned. Let stand 5 minutes. To serve, cut into squares. Yield: 6 servings (1 square per serving).

Sprinkling cornmeal on the pan makes it easier to roll out the dough and adds a nice crunchy texture to the bottom of the baked crust.

Caramelized Onion Pizza

TIME: PREP 19 MINUTES; COOK 15 MINUTES

SELECTIONS

1 PROTEIN/MILK
3 BREAD
1 FRUIT/VEGETABLE
1 FAT

POINTS

7

PER SERVING

332 CALORIES
46.9G CARBOHYDRATE
8.8G FAT (2.8G SATURATED)
3.5G FIBER
16.6G PROTEIN
10MG CHOLESTEROL
672MG SODIUM
231MG CALCIUM
0.9MG IRON

Vegetable cooking spray
2 teaspoons olive oil, divided
2 medium-size purple onions, thinly sliced (about 4 cups)
1 tablespoon brown sugar
¼ teaspoon salt
½ cup water
1 tablespoon minced fresh rosemary
1 tablespoon balsamic vinegar
1 teaspoon cornmeal
1 (10-ounce) can refrigerated pizza dough
1 cup (4 ounces) shredded reduced-fat Jarlsberg cheese

1. Coat a large nonstick skillet with cooking spray; add 1 teaspoon oil. Place over medium heat until hot. Add onion, sugar, and salt; cook 10 minutes, stirring occasionally. Add water; cook 5 minutes or until water evaporates and onion is tender, stirring often. Add rosemary and vinegar; cook 2 minutes or until vinegar evaporates.

2. Coat a large baking sheet with cooking spray; sprinkle with cornmeal. Unroll pizza dough into a 12- x 10-inch rectangle. Cut rectangle into 4 (6- x 5-inch) rectangles. Brush edges of rectangles with remaining 1 teaspoon olive oil. Place rectangles on prepared baking sheet; top evenly with onion mixture, and sprinkle with cheese. Bake at 450° for 15 minutes or until golden. Cut each pizza in half diagonally. Yield: 4 servings (2 wedges per serving).

Caramelizing the onion brings out a sugary sweet flavor, which is the star flavor in this recipe. To make the recipe more versatile, cut each pizza wedge in half, and serve as appetizer pizzas.

Mediterranean-Style Stuffed Eggplant

TIME: PREP 15 MINUTES; COOK 45 MINUTES

2	small eggplants
1	(14½-ounce) can Italian-style stewed tomatoes, undrained
1	cup water
1	tablespoon balsamic vinegar
½	teaspoon dried marjoram
¼	teaspoon ground allspice
1½	cups couscous, uncooked
	Vegetable cooking spray
5	ounces (about 1 cup) crumbled feta cheese with black peppercorns

SELECTIONS

1 PROTEIN/MILK

1 BREAD

2 FRUIT/VEGETABLE

POINTS

5

PER SERVING

233 CALORIES

31.3G CARBOHYDRATE

8.1G FAT (5.3G SATURATED)

3.1G FIBER

10.4G PROTEIN

32MG CHOLESTEROL

681MG SODIUM

226MG CALCIUM

1.5MG IRON

1. Prick each eggplant several times with a fork. Place eggplant on a baking sheet, and bake at 350° for 20 minutes. Let cool. Cut each eggplant in half lengthwise; scoop out pulp, leaving ¼-inch-thick shells. Chop pulp; set shells and pulp aside.

2. Combine tomato and next 4 ingredients in a medium saucepan; bring to a boil, and stir in couscous. Cover, remove from heat, and let stand 5 minutes. Fluff with a fork, and stir in eggplant pulp.

3. Spoon couscous mixture evenly into eggplant shells; place in a 13- x 9- x 2-inch baking dish coated with cooking spray. Top evenly with cheese. Cover and bake at 350° for 25 minutes or until thoroughly heated. Yield: 4 servings.

Couscous is tiny beadlike pasta that's traditional in Mediterranean cuisine. It soaks up the fresh flavors of ingredients like tomatoes, balsamic vinegar, and herbs.

Sesame Vegetable Tofu Stir-Fry

TIME: PREP 11 MINUTES; STAND 50 MINUTES; COOK 9 MINUTES

SELECTIONS

1 PROTEIN/MILK

2 BREAD

1 FRUIT/VEGETABLE

1 FAT

POINTS

6

PER SERVING

310 CALORIES

44.1G CARBOHYDRATE

10.2G FAT (1.6G SATURATED)

5.2G FIBER

11.5G PROTEIN

0MG CHOLESTEROL

423MG SODIUM

139MG CALCIUM

5.4MG IRON

1   (10½-ounce) package extra firm tofu

¼   cup low-sodium soy sauce

1   tablespoon peeled, grated gingerroot

2   teaspoons sugar

2   teaspoons dark sesame oil

2   cloves garlic, minced

2   teaspoons vegetable oil

2   cups fresh broccoli flowerets

1   cup thinly sliced sweet red pepper

2   cups thinly sliced napa cabbage

1   cup fresh bean sprouts

2   teaspoons sesame seeds, toasted

3   cups hot cooked brown rice (cooked without salt or fat)

When tofu is pressed for a few minutes to extract excess liquid, it absorbs even more of the soy sauce, ginger-root, and garlic seasonings.

1. Place tofu between 2 flat plates or cutting boards. Weight the top with a heavy can (sides of tofu should be bulging slightly, but not cracking). Let stand 40 to 45 minutes; pour off liquid, and discard. Cut tofu into ½-inch cubes, and set aside.

2. Combine soy sauce and next 4 ingredients in a medium bowl, stirring well. Add tofu, and toss to coat. Let stand 10 minutes. Remove tofu from marinade, reserving marinade.

3. Drizzle vegetable oil around top of wok, coating sides. Heat at medium-high (375°) until hot. Add tofu, and stir-fry 4 minutes. Add broccoli and red pepper; stir-fry 2 minutes. Add cabbage and bean sprouts, and stir-fry 2 additional minutes or until vegetables are crisp-tender. Add reserved marinade; toss gently, and cook 30 seconds or until thoroughly heated. Stir in sesame seeds.

4. Spoon ¾ cup rice onto each individual serving plate. Top evenly with vegetable mixture. Yield: 4 servings.

Spaghetti Squash with Tomatoes and Beans

TIME: PREP 19 MINUTES; COOK 60 MINUTES

1   (2½-pound) spaghetti squash
Vegetable cooking spray
1   (15-ounce) can salsa-style chunky tomatoes, undrained
1   (15-ounce) can black beans, rinsed and drained
¾   cup (3 ounces) shredded reduced-fat Monterey Jack cheese, divided
¼   cup minced fresh cilantro
1   teaspoon ground cumin
¼   teaspoon ground pepper
Fresh cilantro leaves (optional)

SELECTIONS

1 PROTEIN/MILK
1 BREAD
1 FRUIT/VEGETABLE

POINTS

5

PER SERVING

232 CALORIES
32.4G CARBOHYDRATE
5.4G FAT (2.5G SATURATED)
4.7G FIBER
14.4G PROTEIN
11MG CHOLESTEROL
902MG SODIUM
223MG CALCIUM
3.1MG IRON

1. Wash squash; cut in half lengthwise. Remove and discard seeds. Place squash halves, cut side down, in a 13- x 9- x 2-inch baking dish coated with cooking spray. Add water to depth of ½ inch. Bake at 375° for 25 minutes or until squash is tender; let cool slightly. Using a fork, remove spaghetti-like strands; discard shells.

2. Combine squash strands, tomato, beans, ½ cup cheese, ¼ cup cilantro, cumin, and pepper in a large bowl, stirring well. Spoon into a 1½-quart casserole coated with cooking spray. Sprinkle with remaining ¼ cup cheese.

3. Bake, uncovered, at 350° for 35 minutes or until thoroughly heated. Garnish with cilantro leaves, if desired. Serve immediately. Yield: 4 servings.

You can save time by cooking spaghetti squash in the microwave. Place seeded squash halves, cut side down, in a baking dish. Prick the skin with a fork, and add ¼ cup water to dish. Cover with plastic wrap, and cook at HIGH 7 to 10 minutes or until tender.

Pasta Caponata

TIME: PREP 10 MINUTES; COOK 35 MINUTES

SELECTIONS

2 BREAD

2 FRUIT/VEGETABLE

POINTS

4

PER SERVING

265 CALORIES

52.7G CARBOHYDRATE

2.3G FAT (0.5G SATURATED)

5.6G FIBER

10.1G PROTEIN

1MG CHOLESTEROL

217MG SODIUM

118MG CALCIUM

3.8MG IRON

Olive oil-flavored vegetable cooking spray

2   cups cubed eggplant

1½   cups cubed yellow squash

¾   cup celery

½   cup coarsely chopped onion

2   cloves garlic, minced

2   cups sliced fresh mushrooms

2   (14½-ounce) cans no-salt-added whole tomatoes, undrained
       and chopped

¼   cup chopped pimiento-stuffed olives

1   tablespoon balsamic vinegar

1   tablespoon no-salt-added tomato paste

1   teaspoon dried oregano

½   teaspoon ground pepper

¼   teaspoon salt

6   cups hot cooked penne (tubular pasta),
       cooked without salt or fat

2   tablespoons grated Parmesan cheese

Penne (pen-nay) pasta looks like straightened tubes of large maca-roni. It will take about 11 ounces of dried pasta to equal 6 cups of cooked penne.

1. Coat a 15- x 10- x 1-inch jellyroll pan with cooking spray. Arrange eggplant and squash in pan in a single layer; coat with cooking spray. Broil 5½ inches from heat (with electric oven door partially opened) 7 to 8 minutes or until tender, stirring occasionally. Set aside.

2. Coat a Dutch oven with cooking spray; place over medium-high heat until hot. Add celery, onion, and garlic; cook, stirring constantly, 4 to 5 minutes or until tender. Add mushrooms; cook 4 minutes. Stir in tomato and next 6 ingredients; bring to a boil. Reduce heat, and simmer, uncovered, 20 minutes or until slightly thickened. Stir in eggplant and squash. Serve over pasta, and sprinkle with cheese. Yield: 6 servings.

Ratatouille Rigatoni *(photo, page 77)*

TIME: PREP 12 MINUTES; COOK 23 MINUTES

8   ounces rigatoni (tubular pasta), uncooked

Vegetable cooking spray

1   teaspoon olive oil

3   medium zucchini, sliced

1   medium-size green pepper, sliced

1   (8-ounce) package sliced fresh mushrooms

1   (14½-ounce) can no-salt-added stewed tomatoes, undrained

1   (8-ounce) can no-salt-added tomato sauce

1   teaspoon dried oregano

½   teaspoon ground pepper

¼   teaspoon salt

1   clove garlic, minced

1   bay leaf

2   tablespoons plus 2 teaspoons freshly grated Parmesan cheese

SELECTIONS

3 BREAD

3 FRUIT/VEGETABLE

POINTS

6

PER SERVING

352 CALORIES

62.6G CARBOHYDRATE

5.3G FAT (2.0G SATURATED)

4.9G FIBER

15.4G PROTEIN

7MG CHOLESTEROL

347MG SODIUM

197MG CALCIUM

5.2MG IRON

1. Cook pasta according to package directions, omitting salt and fat. Drain and set aside.

2. Coat a large nonstick skillet with cooking spray; add oil. Place over medium-high heat until hot. Add zucchini, green pepper, and mushrooms; cook 8 minutes or until crisp-tender, stirring often. Add tomato and next 6 ingredients. Cover, reduce heat, and simmer 10 minutes. Uncover and simmer 5 minutes or until slightly thickened. Remove and discard bay leaf.

3. Combine pasta and tomato mixture in a large bowl; toss well. To serve, spoon into individual serving bowls. Sprinkle 2 teaspoons Parmesan cheese over each serving. Yield: 4 servings.

Eight ounces of uncooked rigatoni equals about 2½ cups of dried noodles. Penne pasta is a good substitute for rigatoni; they're similar in size and shape.

Spinach-Stuffed Pasta Shells

TIME: PREP 20 MINUTES; COOK 35 MINUTES

SELECTIONS

1 PROTEIN/MILK

1 BREAD

2 FRUIT/VEGETABLE

40 BONUS CALORIES

POINTS

5

PER SERVING

274 CALORIES

37.9G CARBOHYDRATE

6.6G FAT (3.7G SATURATED)

6.0G FIBER

18.3G PROTEIN

18MG CHOLESTEROL

883MG SODIUM

348MG CALCIUM

3.5MG IRON

1   (26-ounce) jar fat-free spaghetti sauce, divided

Vegetable cooking spray

1   (10-ounce) package frozen chopped spinach, thawed and
       drained

1   cup lite ricotta cheese

½   cup finely shredded Parmesan cheese, divided

½   teaspoon ground pepper

⅛   teaspoon ground nutmeg

12   cooked jumbo pasta shells, cooked without salt or fat

1. Spoon half of spaghetti sauce into an 11- x 7- x 1½-inch baking dish coated with cooking spray. Set aside.

2. Combine spinach, ricotta cheese, ¼ cup Parmesan cheese, pepper, and nutmeg; stir well. Spoon spinach mixture evenly into pasta shells. Arrange shells over sauce in baking dish. Spoon remaining half of spaghetti sauce over shells.

3. Cover and bake at 400° for 35 minutes or until bubbly. Sprinkle with remaining ¼ cup Parmesan cheese. Yield: 4 servings.

Spaghetti sauce from a jar makes this recipe super simple. And, if you buy the already-shredded fresh Parmesan cheese from the refrigerated dairy section, you'll have only one bowl and one spoon to wash when you pop the dish in the oven.

Hoppin' John Skillet Cakes

TIME: PREP 17 MINUTES; COOK 14 MINUTES

1	(15.8-ounce) can black-eyed peas, rinsed and drained
¼	cup plus 3 tablespoons fine, dry breadcrumbs, divided
½	cup sliced green onions
¼	cup fat-free egg substitute
2	teaspoons chili powder
½	teaspoon ground cumin
¼	teaspoon ground red pepper
¼	teaspoon salt
1½	cups cooked brown rice (cooked without salt or fat)

Vegetable cooking spray

2	teaspoons vegetable oil
1	cup no-salt-added salsa
½	cup low-fat sour cream
2	tablespoons minced fresh cilantro

SELECTIONS

2 BREAD

1 FRUIT/VEGETABLE

1 FAT

POINTS

6

PER SERVING

323 CALORIES

48.1G CARBOHYDRATE

12.2G FAT (3.0G SATURATED)

6.9G FIBER

13.2G PROTEIN

11MG CHOLESTEROL

876MG SODIUM

137MG CALCIUM

3.1MG IRON

1. Position knife blade in food processor bowl; add peas, 3 tablespoons breadcrumbs, and next 6 ingredients. Process 30 seconds or until smooth, stopping once to scrape down sides. Add brown rice; pulse 4 times or just until blended.

2. For skillet cakes, shape pea mixture into 8 (½-inch-thick) patties, using ⅓ cup pea mixture for each cake; dredge in remaining ¼ cup breadcrumbs. Coat a large nonstick skillet with cooking spray; add 1 teaspoon oil. Place over medium-high heat until hot. Place 4 patties in skillet, and cook 3½ minutes on each side or until browned. Repeat procedure with remaining 1 teaspoon oil and 4 patties.

3. To serve, spread ¼ cup salsa on each of 4 plates; arrange 2 cakes over salsa on each plate. Top each cake with 1 tablespoon sour cream; sprinkle cilantro over sour cream. Yield: 4 servings (2 cakes, ¼ cup salsa, and 2 tablespoons sour cream per serving).

We found that canned black-eyed peas made from fresh peas tasted much better than those made from dried peas. Check the label to find out which kind you're buying.

Rice-Crusted Pizza Neopolitan

TIME: PREP 20 MINUTES; COOK 15 MINUTES

SELECTIONS

1 PROTEIN/MILK

1 BREAD

2 FRUIT/VEGETABLE

POINTS

6

PER SERVING

330 CALORIES

51.5G CARBOHYDRATE

7.0G FAT (3.0G SATURATED)

4.1G FIBER

14.8G PROTEIN

16MG CHOLESTEROL

611MG SODIUM

231MG CALCIUM

3.2MG IRON

3	cups cooked long-grain rice (cooked without salt or fat)
¼	cup freshly grated Parmesan cheese
¼	cup fat-free egg substitute
	Vegetable cooking spray
1	medium onion, sliced and separated into rings
1	medium-size sweet red pepper, thinly sliced
2	cups sliced fresh mushrooms
2	cloves garlic, minced
1	cup pizza sauce
¾	cup (3 ounces) shredded part-skim mozzarella cheese

1. Combine first 3 ingredients; mix well. Press rice mixture firmly into a 12-inch pizza pan coated with cooking spray. Bake at 425° for 15 minutes. Set aside.

2. Coat a large nonstick skillet with cooking spray; place over medium-high heat until hot. Add onion and pepper; cook 5 minutes or until crisp-tender, stirring often. Add mushrooms and garlic; cook 5 minutes, stirring often.

3. Spread pizza sauce over crust; spoon vegetables over sauce. Sprinkle with cheese. Bake at 425° for 10 minutes or until cheese is melted and lightly browned. Yield: 4 servings.

> If you prefer a quick, more traditional crust, just purchase a 12-inch round packaged flatbread and use the same toppings. Try to use freshly grated Parmesan cheese, rather than the kind in a can, for a big flavor boost.

meats

Picadillo-Stuffed Peppers

TIME: PREP 10 MINUTES; COOK 31 MINUTES

4	large green peppers
6	ounces ground round
1	cup chopped onion
2	cloves garlic, minced
2	cups cooked brown rice (cooked without salt or fat)
1	(8-ounce) can no-salt-added tomato sauce
¼	cup currants or raisins
¼	cup sliced pimiento-stuffed green olives
2	teaspoons chili powder
1	teaspoon ground cumin
¼	teaspoon ground cinnamon

1. Cut tops off peppers, and remove seeds. Cook tops and bottoms of peppers in boiling water 5 minutes. Drain peppers; set aside.

2. Cook ground round, onion, and garlic in a large nonstick skillet over medium heat until meat is browned, stirring until it crumbles; drain. Wipe drippings from skillet with a paper towel. Return meat mixture to skillet, and add rice and remaining 6 ingredients. Cook 3 minutes or until thoroughly heated, stirring occasionally.

3. Spoon meat mixture evenly into pepper shells, and replace tops; place stuffed peppers in an 8-inch square baking dish. Add hot water to dish to depth of 1 inch. Bake, uncovered, at 350° for 20 minutes. Yield: 4 servings.

Use quick-cooking rice instead of regular long-grain brown rice; the quick-cooking variety cooks in only 10 minutes.

Beef and Pepper Stir-Fry

TIME: PREP 8 MINUTES; COOK 12 MINUTES

1   pound lean boneless sirloin steak
½   teaspoon dried rosemary, crushed
½   teaspoon ground pepper
¼   teaspoon salt
2   cloves garlic, minced
Vegetable cooking spray
3   medium-size green peppers, seeded and cut into
       ¼-inch-wide strips
1   teaspoon olive oil
1   tablespoon balsamic vinegar

1. Partially freeze steak; trim fat. Slice steak diagonally across grain into ¼-inch-thick strips; cut strips into 2-inch pieces. Combine rosemary and next 3 ingredients in a large heavy-duty, zip-top plastic bag. Add steak; seal bag, and shake to coat steak. Refrigerate 15 minutes, turning bag once.

2. Coat a large nonstick skillet with cooking spray, and place over medium-high heat until hot. Add pepper strips; cook 6 minutes or until tender, stirring often. Remove from skillet; set aside.

3. Add oil to skillet, and place over medium-high heat until hot. Add steak; cook 4 minutes, stirring often. Return pepper strips to skillet, and add vinegar. Cook 2 minutes or until thoroughly heated. Serve immediately. Yield: 4 servings.

The secret to tender strips of beef is to cut the steak across the grain when you slice it into strips. For a more colorful dish, use a sweet red pepper, a yellow pepper, and a green pepper instead of 3 green peppers.

SELECTIONS

3 PROTEIN/MILK

1 FRUIT/VEGETABLE

POINTS

4

PER SERVING

198 CALORIES

7.0G CARBOHYDRATE

7.6G FAT (2.4G SATURATED)

2.0G FIBER

25.1G PROTEIN

69MG CHOLESTEROL

216MG SODIUM

21MG CALCIUM

4.6MG IRON

Ginger-Grilled Sirloin Steak

TIME: PREP 10 MINUTES; MARINATE 8 HOURS; COOK 15 MINUTES

SELECTIONS

3 PROTEIN/MILK

POINTS

4

PER SERVING

190 CALORIES

2.1G CARBOHYDRATE

7.5G FAT (2.5G SATURATED)

0.0G FIBER

25.9G PROTEIN

76MG CHOLESTEROL

252MG SODIUM

11MG CALCIUM

2.9MG IRON

1	pound lean boneless sirloin steak
¼	cup canned low-sodium beef broth
¼	cup reduced-sodium soy sauce
2	tablespoons peeled, grated gingerroot
1	tablespoon sugar
2	teaspoons sesame oil
2	cloves garlic, minced

Vegetable cooking spray

1. Trim fat from steak. Combine broth and next 5 ingredients in a large heavy-duty, zip-top plastic bag. Add steak; seal bag, and turn bag to coat steak. Marinate in refrigerator at least 8 hours, turning bag occasionally.

2. Remove steak from marinade; discard marinade. Coat grill rack with cooking spray; place on grill over medium-hot coals (350° to 400°). Place steak on rack; grill, covered, 5 to 6 minutes on each side or to desired degree of doneness. Let steak stand 5 minutes. Cut into 4 pieces. Yield: 4 servings.

Keep fresh gingerroot tightly wrapped, and store it in your freezer. Then you can grate it while it's still frozen whenever you need a sweet-hot bite of ginger flavor.

Port Marinated Steak

TIME: PREP 3 MINUTES; MARINATE 8 HOURS; COOK 10 MINUTES

1½ pounds lean boneless top sirloin steak
½ cup port or sweet red wine
2 tablespoons Worcestershire sauce
2 tablespoons balsamic vinegar
2 cloves garlic, crushed
3 tablespoons minced fresh thyme
Vegetable cooking spray

1. Trim fat from steak. Combine wine and next 4 ingredients in a heavy-duty, zip-top plastic bag. Add steak; seal bag, and turn bag to coat steak. Marinate in refrigerator 8 hours, turning bag occasionally.

2. Remove steak from marinade; pour marinade into a small saucepan. Bring marinade to a boil; boil until reduced to ¼ cup. Set aside.

3. Coat grill rack with cooking spray; place on grill over medium-hot coals (350° to 400°). Place steak on rack; grill, covered, 5 minutes on each side or to desired degree of doneness. Let steak stand 5 minutes. Cut diagonally across grain into thin slices; drizzle with marinade. Yield: 6 servings.

SELECTIONS

3 PROTEIN/MILK

POINTS

4

PER SERVING

191 CALORIES

3.6G CARBOHYDRATE

6.7G FAT (2.6G SATURATED)

1.2G FIBER

27.9G PROTEIN

80MG CHOLESTEROL

111MG SODIUM

53MG CALCIUM

4.6MG IRON

Steak marinated in port, a sweet red wine with a bit of brandy added to it, takes on an especially unique flavor. The steak will taste fine if you substitute another sweet red wine, but use port for special occasions.

Beef Filets with Vegetables *(photo, opposite page)*

TIME: PREP 12 MINUTES; COOK 19 MINUTES

Vegetable cooking spray

1	teaspoon olive oil
2	medium-size sweet red peppers, seeded and cut into thin strips
2	medium zucchini, thinly sliced
1	small onion, thinly sliced
1	cup canned no-salt-added beef broth, divided
2	teaspoons minced fresh thyme or ½ teaspoon dried thyme
2	teaspoons all-purpose flour
4	(4-ounce) beef tenderloin steaks (about 1 inch thick)
2	large cloves garlic, halved
½	teaspoon freshly ground pepper

1. Coat a large nonstick skillet with cooking spray; add oil. Place over medium-high heat until hot. Add pepper strips, zucchini, and onion; cook 5 minutes, stirring often. Add ½ cup broth and thyme. Cover, reduce heat, and simmer 5 minutes.

2. Combine remaining ½ cup broth and flour, stirring well with a wire whisk. Add to vegetable mixture, stirring well. Cook, stirring constantly, until slightly thickened and bubbly.

3. Rub steaks with garlic halves; sprinkle with ½ teaspoon pepper. Coat grill rack with cooking spray; place on grill over medium-hot coals (350° to 400°). Place steak on rack; grill, covered, 4 minutes on each side or to desired degree of doneness. Spoon vegetables evenly onto individual serving plates; arrange steaks over vegetables. Yield: 4 servings.

Beef broth provides the base for a quick, rich sauce to complement smoke-scented grilled steaks. Add a salad, and you have a meal.

Cheese-Stuffed Veal Marsala
(recipe, page 101)

Pork and Vegetables in Dijon
Sauce (*recipe, page 105*)

Quick Lamb
Bourguignon
(recipe, page 106)

Skillet Beef Stroganoff

TIME: PREP 8 MINUTES; COOK 23 MINUTES

1   (12-ounce) lean boneless round steak
Vegetable cooking spray
1   large onion, sliced
2   cups sliced fresh mushrooms
¾   cup water
1   tablespoon all-purpose flour
1   tablespoon sweet Hungarian paprika
½   teaspoon beef-flavored bouillon granules
½   cup low-fat sour cream
¼   teaspoon salt
½   teaspoon ground pepper
3   cups hot cooked wide egg noodles (cooked without salt or fat)
Minced fresh parsley (optional)

1. Partially freeze steak; trim fat. Slice steak diagonally across grain into very thin strips; cut strips into 2-inch pieces.

2. Coat a large nonstick skillet with cooking spray; place over medium-high heat until hot. Add steak, and cook 5 minutes or until browned on all sides. Remove steak from skillet; drain. Wipe drippings from skillet with a paper towel. Coat skillet with cooking spray. Add onion; cook, stirring constantly, 5 minutes. Add mushrooms; cook, stirring constantly, 3 minutes. Combine water, flour, paprika, and bouillon granules, stirring until smooth; add to skillet. Stir in steak. Reduce heat to medium-low; cook, stirring constantly, until mixture reaches a simmer. Cook, uncovered, 10 minutes, stirring occasionally.

3. Remove skillet from heat; stir in sour cream, salt, and pepper. To serve, spoon ¾ cup noodles onto each serving plate; spoon beef mixture evenly over noodles. Sprinkle with minced parsley, if desired. Yield: 4 servings.

SELECTIONS

2 PROTEIN/MILK

2 BREAD

1 FRUIT/VEGETABLE

POINTS

7

PER SERVING

368 CALORIES

40.3G CARBOHYDRATE

10.1G FAT (4.1G SATURATED)

4.6G FIBER

28.7G PROTEIN

105MG CHOLESTEROL

334MG SODIUM

67MG CALCIUM

4.9MG IRON

Place steak in the freezer for just 15 minutes to make it firm enough to cut into thin slices for this family favorite. The thinner the slices, the more tender the cooked meat will be.

Beef with Peanut Sauce

TIME: PREP 15 MINUTES; COOK 10 MINUTES

SELECTIONS

2 PROTEIN/MILK

1 BREAD

1 FRUIT/VEGETABLE

90 BONUS CALORIES

POINTS

7

PER SERVING

313 CALORIES

26.6G CARBOHYDRATE

13.0G FAT (4.5G SATURATED)

1.5G FIBER

19.3G PROTEIN

42MG CHOLESTEROL

459MG SODIUM

106MG CALCIUM

2.3MG IRON

1	(1-pound) lean flank steak
2	tablespoons plus 2 teaspoons low-sodium soy sauce, divided
1	teaspoon sesame oil
⅛	teaspoon dried crushed red pepper
6	green onions, cut into 1½-inch pieces
1	(5-ounce) package Japanese curly noodles
3	cups thinly sliced napa cabbage
½	cup evaporated skimmed milk
½	cup canned no-salt-added beef broth
3	tablespoons reduced-fat peanut butter
2	tablespoons peeled, minced gingerroot
1	teaspoon sugar
2	cloves garlic

1. Partially freeze steak; trim fat. Slice steak diagonally across grain into very thin strips; cut strips into 2-inch pieces. Combine 1 tablespoon soy sauce and next 3 ingredients in a large heavy-duty, zip-top plastic bag. Add steak; seal bag, and turn to coat steak. Set aside.

2. Prepare noodles according to package directions, omitting salt and fat; add cabbage to boiling noodles during last minute of cooking time. Drain well, and keep warm. Place remaining 1 tablespoon plus 2 teaspoons soy sauce, milk, and remaining 5 ingredients in container of an electric blender or food processor. Cover and process until smooth; set sauce aside.

3. Place a large nonstick skillet over medium-high heat until hot. Add meat mixture, and cook 3 minutes; remove meat mixture from skillet, and drain. Place sauce in skillet, and cook over medium heat until slightly thickened. Return meat mixture to skillet; cook until heated. Arrange noodle mixture on 6 individual serving plates; top evenly with meat mixture. Serve immediately. Yield: 6 servings.

The crinkly, crisp leaves of napa (or Chinese) cabbage have a delicate, mild flavor that blends well with the peppery, peanut flavor of this easy stir-fry.

Cheese-Stuffed Veal Marsala *(photo, page 96)*

TIME: PREP 14 MINUTES; COOK 21 MINUTES

4   (3-ounce) lean boneless veal chops (1 inch thick)
½   cup grated Romano cheese
2   tablespoons minced fresh oregano
2   tablespoons all-purpose flour
½   teaspoon freshly ground pepper
¼   teaspoon salt
1   teaspoon olive oil
½   cup canned no-salt-added beef broth
¼   cup dry Marsala or other dry red wine
Fresh oregano sprigs (optional)

SELECTIONS

3 PROTEIN/MILK

70 BONUS CALORIES

POINTS

3

PER SERVING

214 CALORIES

4.6G CARBOHYDRATE

8.7G FAT (3.6G SATURATED)

0.3G FIBER

27.7G PROTEIN

105MG CHOLESTEROL

414MG SODIUM

177MG CALCIUM

1.5MG IRON

1. Cut chops in half horizontally to within ½ inch of 1 long edge. Open chops, and place between 2 sheets of heavy-duty plastic wrap; flatten to ¼-inch thickness, using a meat mallet or rolling pin.

2. Combine cheese and minced oregano, tossing lightly; place one-fourth of mixture on 1 cut half of each veal chop. Fold chops to enclose filling; press edges together, and secure with wooden picks.

3. Combine flour, pepper, and salt in a shallow dish; coat chops on all sides with mixture.

4. Pour oil into a large nonstick skillet; place over medium-high heat until hot. Add chops to skillet; cook 3 minutes on each side or until browned. Add broth and wine; bring to a boil. Reduce heat, and simmer, uncovered, 15 minutes, turning chops occasionally.

5. To serve, place chops on individual serving plates; spoon pan juices over chops. Garnish with oregano sprigs, if desired. Yield: 4 servings.

These veal chops stuffed with herbed cheese and cooked in wine made a hit with our staff. Veal is expensive, but the flavor of this recipe is worth every penny.

Hot Peppered Pork

TIME: PREP 15 MINUTES; COOK 11 MINUTES

SELECTIONS

3 PROTEIN/MILK

1 FRUIT/VEGETABLE

POINTS

5

PER SERVING

212 CALORIES

4.3G CARBOHYDRATE

10.2G FAT (3.2G SATURATED)

1.3G FIBER

24.8G PROTEIN

68MG CHOLESTEROL

210MG SODIUM

73MG CALCIUM

2.0MG IRON

1	pound lean boneless pork loin
1	tablespoon low-sodium soy sauce
	Vegetable cooking spray
1	medium-size sweet red pepper, seeded and sliced into thin strips
1	teaspoon vegetable oil
2	teaspoons peeled, grated gingerroot
½	teaspoon dried crushed red pepper
2	cloves garlic, minced
¼	cup canned no-salt-added beef broth
4	cups shredded napa cabbage

1. Partially freeze pork; trim fat. Slice pork into ¼-inch-thick strips; cut strips into 2-inch pieces. Combine pork and soy sauce in a large heavy-duty, zip-top plastic bag; seal bag, and turn to coat pork. Let stand 5 minutes.

2. Coat a large nonstick skillet with cooking spray, and place over medium-high heat until hot. Add sweet red pepper; cook 3 minutes or until crisp-tender, stirring often. Remove from skillet, and set aside.

3. Add oil to skillet; place over medium-high heat until hot. Add gingerroot, crushed red pepper, and garlic; cook, stirring constantly, 30 seconds. Add pork to skillet; cook 5 minutes or until pork is done, stirring often. Add sweet red pepper and broth to skillet; bring to a boil. Reduce heat, and simmer 2 to 3 minutes or until most of liquid is evaporated.

4. Place 1 cup shredded cabbage on each of 4 individual serving plates. Spoon pork mixture evenly over cabbage. Serve immediately. Yield: 4 servings.

Ginger, garlic, and dried crushed red pepper give pork strips a sweet-hot bite. Serve the tender pork over a bed of cool, crunchy napa cabbage for a refreshing flavor contrast.

Honey-Cinnamon Pork

TIME: PREP 10 MINUTES; COOK 20 MINUTES

1   (¾-pound) pork tenderloin
1   teaspoon ground white pepper
¼   teaspoon ground cinnamon
¼   teaspoon ground cloves
2   teaspoons olive oil
½   cup sliced carrot (about 2 medium)
2   medium onions, sliced
1   cup sliced fresh green beans
½   cup canned no-salt-added beef broth
3   cloves garlic, minced
2   tablespoons honey
1   teaspoon cornstarch
1   tablespoon water

1. Trim fat from pork; cut into ¼-inch-thick strips. Combine pepper, cinnamon, and cloves in a large heavy-duty, zip-top plastic bag. Add pork; seal bag, and shake to coat pork.

2. Place a large nonstick skillet over high heat until hot, and add oil. Add carrot and onion; cook 3 minutes or until crisp-tender, stirring often. Remove carrot mixture from skillet, using a slotted spoon; set aside.

3. Add pork to skillet; cook 5 minutes or until browned, stirring often. Add carrot mixture, green beans, broth, and garlic to skillet; bring to a boil. Reduce heat to low, and simmer, covered, 10 minutes or until pork is tender.

4. Combine honey and cornstarch in a small bowl; add water, 1 teaspoon at a time, stirring until mixture forms a paste. Add cornstarch mixture to skillet, and cook, stirring constantly, 1 minute or until thickened and bubbly. Yield: 4 servings.

SELECTIONS

3 PROTEIN/MILK

1 FRUIT/VEGETABLE

1 FAT

POINTS

4

PER SERVING

208 CALORIES

22.3G CARBOHYDRATE

4.6G FAT (1.1G SATURATED)

2.9G FIBER

19.8G PROTEIN

55MG CHOLESTEROL

56MG SODIUM

47MG CALCIUM

1.9MG IRON

Cinnamon and cloves have long been traditional seasonings for pork; they bring out the succulent natural sweetness in the meat.

Lemon Pork Scaloppine

TIME: PREP 10 MINUTES; COOK 9 MINUTES

1	(1 pound) pork tenderloin
3	tablespoons all-purpose flour
¼	teaspoon salt
¼	teaspoon pepper
	Vegetable cooking spray
2	teaspoons olive oil, divided
3	tablespoons lemon juice
2	tablespoons water
1	teaspoon capers
¼	cup minced fresh parsley

1. Trim fat from tenderloin. Cut tenderloin into ½-inch-thick slices; place slices between 2 sheets of heavy-duty plastic wrap, and pound to ¼-inch thickness, using a meat mallet or rolling pin.

2. Combine flour, salt, and pepper in a large heavy-duty, zip-top plastic bag; add pork slices. Seal bag, and shake until pork is coated.

3. Coat a large nonstick skillet with cooking spray; add 1 teaspoon oil, and place over medium-high heat until hot. Add half of pork slices; cook 2 minutes on each side or until browned. Transfer to a serving plate; keep warm. Repeat procedure with remaining 1 teaspoon oil and pork slices; remove skillet from heat.

4. Add lemon juice, water, and capers to skillet; bring just to a boil. Pour mixture over pork slices; sprinkle with parsley. Yield: 4 servings.

Here's your answer to the busiest night—an entrée, start to finish, in less than **20** minutes. You can omit the capers, but the vinegary flavor is worth keeping them on hand.

Pork and Vegetables in Dijon Sauce *(photo, page 97)*

TIME: PREP 6 MINUTES; COOK 20 MINUTES

2   (¾-pound) pork tenderloins
Olive oil-flavored vegetable cooking spray
1   teaspoon olive oil
2   cups sliced carrot (about 8 medium)
2   cups broccoli flowerets
1   cup small fresh green beans
1   (8-ounce) package sliced fresh mushrooms
2   cups skim milk
3   tablespoons all-purpose flour
1½   tablespoons Dijon mustard
½   teaspoon salt
¼   teaspoon ground pepper
¼   cup grated Asiago or Parmesan cheese

1. Trim fat from tenderloins. Cut into ½-inch-thick slices. Coat a large nonstick skillet with cooking spray; place over medium-high heat until hot. Add pork slices; cook 2 minutes on each side or until browned; drain and set aside. Wipe drippings from skillet with a paper towel.

2. Coat skillet with cooking spray, and add oil; place over medium-high heat until hot. Add carrot, broccoli, and green beans; cook 4 minutes, stirring often. Add mushrooms to skillet; cook 2 minutes or until tender, stirring often.

3. Combine milk and next 4 ingredients, stirring until smooth. Pour into skillet. Add pork slices, and bring to a boil; reduce heat, and simmer, uncovered, 10 minutes. Add cheese, stirring until smooth. Yield: 6 servings.

SELECTIONS

3 PROTEIN/MILK

1 FRUIT/VEGETABLE

60 BONUS CALORIES

POINTS

5

PER SERVING

236 CALORIES

15.9G CARBOHYDRATE

5.4G FAT (1.8G SATURATED)

3.2G FIBER

30.5G PROTEIN

78MG CHOLESTEROL

486MG SODIUM

183MG CALCIUM

2.8MG IRON

Asiago cheese has a rich, nutty flavor. It's hard, like Parmesan, and easy to grate.

Quick Lamb Bourguignon *(photo, page 98)*

TIME: PREP 5 MINUTES; COOK 25 MINUTES

<u>SELECTIONS</u>

3 PROTEIN/MILK

30 BONUS CALORIES

<u>POINTS</u>

4

<u>PER SERVING</u>

190 CALORIES

7.1G CARBOHYDRATE

6.4G FAT (2.0G SATURATED)

0.5G FIBER

24.3G PROTEIN

73MG CHOLESTEROL

226MG SODIUM

26MG CALCIUM

2.6MG IRON

1	pound lean boneless leg of lamb
	Vegetable cooking spray
1	teaspoon olive oil
1	cup frozen pearl onions, thawed
2	cloves garlic, minced
1	cup canned no-salt-added beef broth
½	cup dry red wine
¼	cup strongly brewed coffee
1½	tablespoons all-purpose flour
1	tablespoon no-salt-added tomato paste
½	teaspoon ground pepper
¼	teaspoon salt

1. Trim fat from lamb. Place lamb between 2 sheets of heavy-duty plastic wrap, and flatten to ½-inch thickness, using a meat mallet or rolling pin; cut into 1-inch pieces.

2. Coat a large nonstick skillet with cooking spray; add oil. Place over medium-high heat until hot. Add lamb; cook 6 minutes or until browned on all sides. Remove meat from skillet; set aside.

3. Add onions to skillet; cook 2 minutes or until lightly browned and tender, stirring often. Add garlic; cook 30 seconds, stirring often. Remove from skillet, and set aside.

4. Pour beef broth and wine into skillet; bring to a boil. Reduce heat, and simmer, uncovered, 5 minutes. Combine coffee and remaining 4 ingredients, stirring until smooth; pour into skillet. Cook, stirring constantly, until sauce is thickened. Add lamb and onion mixture; simmer 10 minutes, stirring occasionally. Yield: 4 servings.

The gravy in this meaty stew is so thick and rich you won't know it's low fat. Wine and strongly brewed coffee blend to make it rich-tasting and flavorful. If you don't like lamb, use beef instead.

Honey Lamb and Vegetables

TIME: PREP 16 MINUTES; STAND 30 MINUTES; COOK 12 MINUTES

1	pound lean boneless leg of lamb
1	small eggplant, peeled (about ¾ pound)
¼	teaspoon salt
Vegetable cooking spray	
2	cups small fresh mushrooms, cut in half
1	medium-size green pepper, seeded and sliced into thin strips
2	tablespoons honey
2	tablespoons low-sodium soy sauce
¼	teaspoon salt
2	cloves garlic, crushed
2	cups hot cooked long-grain rice (cooked without salt or fat)

1. Partially freeze lamb; trim fat. Slice into ¼-inch-thick strips; cut strips into 2-inch pieces. Set aside.

2. Cut eggplant into 1-inch cubes; place eggplant in a colander. Sprinkle with ¼ teaspoon salt, and let stand 30 minutes. Pat dry with paper towels.

3. Coat a large nonstick skillet with cooking spray, and place over medium-high heat until hot. Add lamb; cook 6 minutes or until browned, stirring often. Add mushrooms, pepper strips, and eggplant; cook 5 minutes or until vegetables are tender. Add honey and next 3 ingredients; cook, stirring constantly, 1 minute or until thoroughly heated. Serve over rice. Yield: 4 servings.

SELECTIONS

3 PROTEIN/MILK

1 BREAD

2 FRUIT/VEGETABLE

POINTS

7

PER SERVING

334 CALORIES

42.4G CARBOHYDRATE

5.8G FAT (1.9G SATURATED)

2.8G FIBER

27.4G PROTEIN

73MG CHOLESTEROL

565MG SODIUM

53MG CALCIUM

4.4MG IRON

It's important to sprinkle the eggplant with salt and allow it to stand 30 minutes—the procedure helps to eliminate any bitter taste from the eggplant flesh.

Curried Lamb Kabobs

TIME: PREP 13 MINUTES; MARINATE 2 HOURS; COOK 20 MINUTES

SELECTIONS

3 PROTEIN/MILK

2 FRUIT/VEGETABLE

POINTS

6

PER SERVING

257 CALORIES

14.1G CARBOHYDRATE

9.0G FAT (3.1G SATURATED)

2.2G FIBER

29.5G PROTEIN

81MG CHOLESTEROL

201MG SODIUM

106MG CALCIUM

3.4MG IRON

1   pound lean boneless leg of lamb
½   cup plain nonfat yogurt
1   tablespoon low-sodium soy sauce
1   teaspoon curry powder
2   small onions
1   large green pepper, seeded and cut into 16 pieces
16   medium-size fresh mushrooms
Vegetable cooking spray

1. Trim fat from lamb; cut lamb into 1¼-inch cubes. Place lamb in a shallow dish. Combine yogurt, soy sauce, and curry powder; add to lamb, and stir to coat. Cover and marinate in refrigerator at least 2 hours.

2. Cook onions in boiling water to cover in a medium saucepan 10 minutes. Drain and cut each onion into 4 wedges.

3. Remove lamb from marinade, reserving marinade. Thread lamb, onion, green pepper, and mushrooms alternately onto 8 (10-inch) skewers; brush with reserved marinade.

4. Coat a grill rack with cooking spray; place on grill over medium-hot coals (350° to 400°). Place kabobs on rack; grill, covered, 10 minutes or to desired degree of doneness, turning kabobs once. Serve immediately. Yield: 4 servings.

Curry powder is a blend of 15 or more spices and seeds, so you get a delicious assortment of flavors, including cinnamon, fennel seed, nutmeg, and cumin, from just one spice mix.

Mustard-Garlic Lamb Chops

2 cloves garlic, minced
½ teaspoon ground pepper
¼ teaspoon dried thyme
⅛ teaspoon salt
2 teaspoons fresh lemon juice
2 teaspoons Dijon mustard
1 teaspoon olive oil
4 (5-ounce) lean lamb loin chops (1 inch thick)
Vegetable cooking spray

1. Combine garlic, pepper, thyme, and salt in a small bowl; mash with back of a spoon until mixture forms a paste. Stir in lemon juice, mustard, and olive oil.

2. Trim fat from chops. Spread garlic mixture over both sides of chops. Place chops on rack of a broiler pan coated with cooking spray. Broil 5½ inches from heat (with electric oven door partially opened) 6 to 7 minutes on each side or to desired degree of doneness. Yield: 4 servings.

We assigned our highest flavor rating to this easy recipe. All you do is spread on a paste of spices, Dijon mustard, and lemon juice, and broil the chops.

SELECTIONS

3 PROTEIN/ MILK

POINTS

5

PER SERVING

192 CALORIES
1.1G CARBOHYDRATE
9.3G FAT (3.0G SATURATED)
0.1G FIBER
24.3G PROTEIN
77MG CHOLESTEROL
216MG SODIUM
21MG CALCIUM
1.8MG IRON

Herbed Lamb Chops

TIME: PREP 10 MINUTES; MARINATE 1 HOUR; COOK 15 MINUTES

SELECTIONS

3 PROTEIN/MILK

POINTS

5

PER SERVING

190 CALORIES

4.2G CARBOHYDRATE

7.9G FAT (2.8G SATURATED)

0.2G FIBER

24.0G PROTEIN

76MG CHOLESTEROL

215MG SODIUM

25MG CALCIUM

2.0MG IRON

½	teaspoon dried rosemary, crushed
½	teaspoon ground pepper
¼	teaspoon salt
¼	teaspoon dried oregano
¼	teaspoon rubbed sage
1	clove garlic, minced
4	(5-ounce) lean lamb loin chops (1 inch thick)
¼	cup balsamic vinegar
¼	cup canned no-salt-added beef broth
1	tablespoon sugar
1	teaspoon dried rosemary, crushed

Vegetable cooking spray

1. Combine first 6 ingredients in a small bowl; stir well. Press mixture evenly onto all sides of lamb chops; place chops on a plate. Cover and marinate in refrigerator 1 to 2 hours.

2. Combine vinegar and next 3 ingredients in a small saucepan; bring to a boil over low heat. Cook 1 minute; remove from heat, and let cool. Strain through a wire mesh strainer, reserving liquid.

3. Arrange chops on rack of a broiler pan coated with cooking spray. Broil 5½ inches from heat (with electric oven door partially opened) 7 to 8 minutes on each side or to desired degree of doneness. To serve, spoon vinegar mixture over lamb chops. Yield: 4 servings.

The longer you allow the lamb and herbs to marinate, the stronger the herb flavor will be when the meat is cooked.

poultry

Braised Lemon Chicken

TIME: PREP 12 MINUTES; COOK 30 MINUTES

Vegetable cooking spray

2   teaspoons margarine

1   (3-pound) broiler-fryer, skinned and cut up

1   pound small round red potatoes, quartered

2   cloves garlic, crushed

½   cup fresh lemon juice

¼   cup canned low-sodium chicken broth

2   medium zucchini, sliced

1   tablespoon minced fresh tarragon

1. Coat a large nonstick skillet with cooking spray; add margarine. Place over medium-high heat until hot. Add chicken, and cook 2 minutes on each side or until lightly browned.

2. Add potato and next 3 ingredients; bring to a boil. Cover, reduce heat, and simmer 15 minutes. Add zucchini and tarragon; cover and simmer 10 additional minutes. Yield: 6 servings.

> Braising is the technique of cooking meat and vegetables covered in liquid. It allows seasonings to seep into the food to keep it moist and flavorful. Just be sure to use a tight-fitting lid on your skillet or Dutch oven.

Grilled Chicken Teriyaki *(cover photo)*

TIME: PREP 5 MINUTES; MARINATE 8 HOURS; COOK 20 MINUTES

½   cup low-sodium soy sauce

¼   cup dry white wine

2   tablespoons honey

½   teaspoon ground ginger

2   cloves garlic, minced

6   (6-ounce) skinned chicken breast halves

Vegetable cooking spray

SELECTIONS

3 PROTEIN/MILK

POINTS

4

PER SERVING

178 CALORIES

6.4G CARBOHYDRATE

3.2G FAT (0.9G SATURATED)

0.0G FIBER

27.4G PROTEIN

75MG CHOLESTEROL

585MG SODIUM

16MG CALCIUM

1.0MG IRON

1. Combine first 5 ingredients in a large heavy-duty, zip-top plastic bag; add chicken. Seal bag, and turn to coat chicken. Marinate in refrigerator 8 hours, turning occasionally.

2. Remove chicken from marinade; place marinade in a small saucepan. Bring to a boil; remove from heat, and set aside.

3. Coat grill rack with cooking spray; place on grill over medium-hot coals (350° to 400°). Place chicken on rack, and grill, covered, 20 to 25 minutes or until chicken is tender, turning occasionally and basting with reserved marinade. Yield: 6 servings.

> Soy sauce and ground ginger give a fresh and spicy flavor to this easy make-ahead grilled chicken. Put it in the refrigerator to marinate in the morning, and it'll be ready to grill for supper.

Santa Fe Chicken Ragout *(photo, opposite page)*

TIME: PREP 9 MINUTES; COOK 36 MINUTES

2   teaspoons olive oil, divided
1½   pounds chicken thighs, skinned
1   cup chopped onion
3   cloves garlic, minced
1   (14½-ounce) can Mexican-style stewed tomatoes, undrained
½   cup canned low-sodium chicken broth
½   teaspoon dried oregano
1   (15-ounce) can no-salt-added black beans, drained
1   (8¾-ounce) can no-salt-added whole-kernel corn, drained

1. Add 1 teaspoon oil to a large nonstick skillet; place skillet over medium-high heat until hot. Add chicken; cook 3 to 4 minutes on each side or until browned. Remove chicken from skillet; set aside, and keep warm. Wipe drippings from skillet with a paper towel.

2. Add remaining 1 teaspoon oil to skillet; place over medium heat until hot. Add onion and garlic; cook 5 minutes or until onion is tender, stirring often. Add tomato, chicken broth, and oregano; bring to a boil. Return chicken to skillet; cover, reduce heat, and simmer 15 minutes. Stir in beans and corn. Cover and simmer 10 minutes. Yield: 4 servings.

Several flavors are blended in canned Mexican-style stewed tomatoes to add flavor—not extra ingredients—to recipes. Eat this hearty stew with a fork and a spoon to enjoy every morsel.

Stir-Fried Chicken
and Vegetables
(recipe, page 121)

116

Turkey Quesadillas
(recipe, page 127)

Ginger Chicken
with Couscous
(recipe, page 119)

Basil Chicken
and Vegetables
(*recipe, page 125*)

Ginger Chicken with Couscous *(photo, page 117)*

TIME: PREP 16 MINUTES; COOK 38 MINUTES

Vegetable cooking spray
2   teaspoons margarine
1   cup finely chopped green onions
1   cup chopped green pepper
8   (4-ounce) skinned, boned chicken breast halves
½   cup canned low-sodium chicken broth
½   cup low-sodium soy sauce
2   tablespoons peeled, chopped gingerroot
1   (9-ounce) jar mango chutney
4   cups hot cooked couscous (cooked without salt or fat)
Green onion fans (optional)

1. Coat a large nonstick skillet with cooking spray; add margarine. Place over medium-high heat until margarine melts. Add chopped green onions and pepper; cook 5 minutes or until tender, stirring often. Transfer pepper mixture to a small bowl; set aside.

2. Coat skillet with cooking spray; place over medium heat until hot. Add chicken, and cook 4 minutes on each side or until browned. Combine broth and next 3 ingredients; pour over chicken in skillet. Bring to a boil; cover, reduce heat, and simmer 10 minutes or until chicken is done, turning occasionally. Remove chicken from skillet with a slotted spoon; set aside, and keep warm.

3. Add pepper mixture to skillet; bring to a boil. Reduce heat, and simmer, uncovered, 15 minutes.

4. To serve, place ½ cup couscous on each individual serving plate, and top each serving with a chicken breast half. Spoon pepper mixture evenly over chicken. Garnish with green onion fans, if desired. Yield: 8 servings.

SELECTIONS

3 PROTEIN/MILK

1 BREAD

108 BONUS CALORIES

POINTS

7

PER SERVING

343 CALORIES

44.7G CARBOHYDRATE

2.9G FAT (0.6G SATURATED)

1.5G FIBER

30.2G PROTEIN

66MG CHOLESTEROL

760MG SODIUM

47MG CALCIUM

1.9MG IRON

This recipe was a staff hit. The blend of mango and spice flavors in the chutney made it supereasy, too. If you can't find mango chutney, just use any other fruit chutney.

Spinach-Stuffed Chicken Breasts

TIME: PREP 12 MINUTES; COOK 27 MINUTES

SELECTIONS

3 PROTEIN/MILK

1 FRUIT/VEGETABLE

1 FAT

POINTS

3

PER SERVING

175 CALORIES

5.1G CARBOHYDRATE

4.3G FAT (0.8G SATURATED)

3.2G FIBER

29.6G PROTEIN

66MG CHOLESTEROL

322MG SODIUM

84MG CALCIUM

3.3MG IRON

4	(4-ounce) skinned, boned chicken breast halves
1	(10-ounce) bag fresh spinach
¼	cup water
¼	teaspoon salt
½	teaspoon ground pepper
2	cloves garlic, minced
2	tablespoons dried tomato bits
2	tablespoons pine nuts, toasted
½	teaspoon dried basil, divided

Vegetable cooking spray

⅓ cup dry white wine

1. Place chicken breast halves between 2 sheets of heavy-duty plastic wrap, and flatten to ¼-inch thickness, using a meat mallet or rolling pin. Set aside.

2. Trim and chop spinach; place in a large nonstick skillet over medium-high heat. Add water and next 3 ingredients; bring to a boil. Cook 7 minutes or until spinach wilts, stirring occasionally. Remove from heat; stir in tomato bits, pine nuts, and ¼ teaspoon basil.

3. Divide spinach mixture evenly among chicken breast halves, spooning mixture onto center of each half. Roll chicken up lengthwise, tucking ends under; secure chicken with wooden picks.

4. Coat skillet with cooking spray. Place over medium-high heat until hot. Add chicken, and cook 2 minutes on each side or until browned. Add wine and remaining ¼ teaspoon basil; bring to a boil. Cover, reduce heat, and simmer 20 minutes or until chicken is done. Transfer chicken to a serving platter, and remove wooden picks. Spoon pan drippings over chicken. Yield: 4 servings.

Pine nuts are expensive and sometimes hard to find, but you can get the same crunch and a comparable flavor if you substitute toasted slivered almonds.

Stir-Fried Chicken and Vegetables *(photo, page 116)*

TIME: PREP 15 MINUTES; MARINATE 1 HOUR; COOK 10 MINUTES

1   pound skinned, boned chicken breast halves, cut into
      ¾-inch pieces
1   tablespoon low-sodium soy sauce
2   teaspoons sesame oil, divided
Vegetable cooking spray
2   cups sliced fresh mushrooms
1   cup thinly sliced onion
1   cup thinly sliced carrot
1   clove garlic, minced
2   cups snow pea pods
1   (15-ounce) can whole baby corn, drained

1. Combine chicken, soy sauce, and 1 teaspoon sesame oil in a large heavy-duty, zip-top plastic bag; seal and turn bag to coat chicken. Marinate in refrigerator 1 hour.

2. Coat a wok or large nonstick skillet with cooking spray; heat at medium-high (375°) until hot. Remove chicken from marinade, discarding marinade. Add chicken, and stir-fry 3 minutes or until chicken is browned. Remove chicken from wok, and drain; wipe drippings from wok with paper towels.

3. Coat wok with cooking spray; drizzle remaining 1 teaspoon oil around top of wok, coating sides. Add mushrooms, onion, carrot, and garlic to wok; stir-fry 4 minutes or until carrot is tender. Return chicken to wok; add snow peas and baby corn. Stir-fry 3 minutes or until chicken is done and vegetables are tender. Yield: 4 servings.

SELECTIONS

3 PROTEIN/MILK

2 FRUIT/VEGETABLE

1 FAT

POINTS

4

PER SERVING

231 CALORIES

13.2G CARBOHYDRATE

5.9G FAT (1.2G SATURATED)

4.3G FIBER

29.7G PROTEIN

72MG CHOLESTEROL

181MG SODIUM

50MG CALCIUM

2.5MG IRON

Since this simple stir-fry isn't saucy, we suggest serving it with sticky rice—it's made from short-grain rice that "sticks" together and is easy to eat with a fork.

Spanish Chicken and Rice

TIME: PREP 4 MINUTES; COOK 31 MINUTES

SELECTIONS
2 PROTEIN/MILK
2 BREAD
1 FRUIT/VEGETABLE

POINTS
6

PER SERVING
322 CALORIES
48.5G CARBOHYDRATE
1.7G FAT (0.4G SATURATED)
3.5G FIBER
25.3G PROTEIN
49MG CHOLESTEROL
415MG SODIUM
54MG CALCIUM
3.6MG IRON

Vegetable cooking spray
1 cup chopped onion
1 clove garlic, minced
1 cup long-grain rice, uncooked
½ teaspoon salt
½ teaspoon dried oregano
½ teaspoon ground cumin
½ teaspoon ground pepper
¼ teaspoon ground turmeric
1 (14½-ounce) can no-salt-added diced tomatoes, undrained
1 (14¼-ounce) can no-salt-added chicken broth
3 (4-ounce) skinned, boned chicken breast halves, cut into ¾-inch pieces
½ cup frozen English peas, thawed
1 (2-ounce) jar sliced pimiento, drained

1. Coat a large nonstick skillet with cooking spray; place over medium-high heat until hot. Add onion; cook 5 minutes or until tender, stirring often. Add garlic; cook 1 minute, stirring often. Add rice and next 5 ingredients; cook, stirring constantly, 3 minutes.

2. Stir in tomato, broth, and chicken; bring to a boil. Cover, reduce heat, and simmer 20 minutes without stirring. Add peas, and toss with a fork. Cover and cook 2 minutes. Add pimiento, and toss. Serve hot. Yield: 4 servings.

It takes only 4 minutes of preparation time to make a one-dish meal of chicken, rice, and vegetables. Turmeric is the spice that adds the traditional yellow color to the recipe.

Chutney Chicken Curry

TIME: PREP 4 MINUTES; COOK 20 MINUTES

2 teaspoons margarine

1 cup chopped onion

2 teaspoons curry powder

1 (14½-ounce) can crushed tomatoes, undrained

⅓ cup mango chutney

3 tablespoons white wine vinegar

2 tablespoons honey

¾ pound skinned, boned chicken breast halves, cut into
   1-inch pieces

3 cups hot cooked rice (cooked without salt or fat)

1. Add margarine to a large skillet; place skillet over medium–high heat until margarine melts. Add onion, and cook 3 minutes or until tender, stirring often. Stir in curry powder; cook, stirring constantly, 1 minute.

2. Stir in tomato and next 3 ingredients; bring to a boil. Reduce heat, and simmer 5 minutes.

3. Stir in chicken. Bring to a boil; reduce heat, and simmer 8 to 10 minutes or until chicken is done. Serve over rice. Yield: 4 servings.

Here's an easy skillet chicken dinner to put on the table in less than 30 minutes. Mango chutney is the base for the thick sweet-and-sour sauce that coats the chicken. Substitute another fruit chutney if mango isn't available.

SELECTIONS

3 PROTEIN/MILK

2 BREAD

1 FRUIT/VEGETABLE

1 FAT

110 BONUS CALORIES

POINTS

9

PER SERVING

428 CALORIES

72.4G CARBOHYDRATE

3.5G FAT (0.7G SATURATED)

2.2G FIBER

24.6G PROTEIN

49MG CHOLESTEROL

441MG SODIUM

93MG CALCIUM

3.0MG IRON

Greek Spaghetti with Feta Cheese and Chicken

TIME: PREP 6 MINUTES; COOK 23 MINUTES

SELECTIONS

3 PROTEIN/MILK

1 BREAD

1 FRUIT/VEGETABLE

1 FAT

POINTS

5

PER SERVING

336 CALORIES

39.5G CARBOHYDRATE

6.7G FAT (2.8G SATURATED)

2.3G FIBER

28.6G PROTEIN

62MG CHOLESTEROL

435MG SODIUM

145MG CALCIUM

3.6MG IRON

3   (4-ounce) skinned, boned chicken breast halves

½   cup canned low-sodium chicken broth

1½   teaspoons dried oregano, divided

1   teaspoon olive oil

2   cloves garlic, minced

1   (14½-ounce) can no-salt-added whole tomatoes, chopped

1   tablespoon lemon juice

½   cup thinly sliced green onions

¼   teaspoon salt

6   ounces thin spaghetti, uncooked

2   tablespoons minced fresh parsley

6   kalamata olives, pitted and quartered

2   ounces feta cheese, crumbled

1. Place chicken in a medium saucepan; add chicken broth and ½ teaspoon oregano. Bring to a boil; cover, reduce heat, and simmer 10 minutes. Remove chicken from broth; transfer to a plate to cool. Shred chicken with a fork, and return to broth.

2. Pour oil into a large nonstick skillet; place over medium heat until hot. Add garlic, and cook 2 minutes, stirring often. Add tomato, lemon juice, and remaining 1 teaspoon oregano. Stir in chicken mixture. Bring to a boil; reduce heat, and simmer, uncovered, 5 minutes. Stir in green onions and salt; remove from heat.

3. Cook pasta according to package directions, omitting salt and fat; drain and place in a large bowl. Add chicken mixture, parsley, olives, and cheese; toss well. Serve immediately. Yield: 4 servings.

For extra flavor try one of the new flavored feta cheeses like black peppercorn or tomato-basil.

Basil Chicken and Vegetables *(photo, page 118)*

TIME: PREP 14 MINUTES; COOK 30 MINUTES

Vegetable cooking spray

4	(4-ounce) skinned, boned chicken breast halves, cut into 1-inch strips
1	large sweet red pepper, thinly sliced
1	small zucchini, sliced
⅔	cup thinly sliced carrot
½	cup tightly packed shredded fresh basil
½	teaspoon ground black pepper
1	tablespoon plus 1 teaspoon olive oil
¼	cup freshly grated Parmesan cheese

SELECTIONS

3 PROTEIN/MILK

1 FRUIT/VEGETABLE

1 FAT

POINTS

5

PER SERVING

219 CALORIES

5.6G CARBOHYDRATE

8.3G FAT (2.2G SATURATED)

1.5G FIBER

29.7G PROTEIN

71MG CHOLESTEROL

196MG SODIUM

114MG CALCIUM

1.8MG IRON

1. Tear off 4 (12-inch) lengths of heavy-duty aluminum foil; fold each piece of foil in half, shiny sides together. Place on a baking sheet, and open out flat, shiny side up. Coat with cooking spray.

2. Arrange one-fourth of chicken strips on half of each aluminum foil square near the crease. Spoon vegetables evenly over chicken; sprinkle with basil and ground pepper. Drizzle 1 teaspoon olive oil over vegetables in each packet. Fold aluminum foil over chicken and vegetables, bringing edges together; fold edges over to seal securely. Pleat and crimp edges to make an airtight seal. Bake at 375° for 30 minutes.

3. Remove chicken mixture from packets, and transfer to individual serving plates. Or, if desired, place packets on individual serving plates; cut an opening in the top of each packet, and fold aluminum foil back. Sprinkle each serving with 1 tablespoon Parmesan cheese. Serve immediately. Yield: 4 servings.

Fill foil packets with chicken and vegetables the night before, and they'll be ready to bake or grill. You can grill the packets over medium-hot coals (350° to 400°) for **20** minutes.

Sesame Chicken

TIME: PREP 2 MINUTES; COOK 11 MINUTES

SELECTIONS

3 PROTEIN/MILK

1 BREAD

90 BONUS CALORIES

POINTS

7

PER SERVING

328 CALORIES

43.0G CARBOHYDRATE

2.8G FAT (0.6G SATURATED)

0.8G FIBER

29.2G PROTEIN

66MG CHOLESTEROL

428MG SODIUM

34MG CALCIUM

2.1MG IRON

1	tablespoon sesame seeds
1	cup canned no-salt-added chicken broth
½	cup dry sherry
1	pound chicken breast tenders
¼	cup red pepper jelly
2	tablespoons low-sodium soy sauce
2	tablespoons water
1½	tablespoons cornstarch
¼	teaspoon salt
2	cups hot cooked long-grain rice (cooked without salt or fat)
⅓	cup sliced green onions

If you don't have leftover rice, use quick-cooking rice and put it on to cook while the chicken simmers.

1. Place sesame seeds in a heavy nonstick skillet over medium-high heat. Cook, stirring constantly, until toasted. Remove seeds, and set aside.

2. Pour broth and sherry into skillet; bring to a boil. Add chicken; cover, reduce heat, and simmer 8 to 10 minutes or until chicken is tender. Remove chicken from skillet with a slotted spoon; set aside.

3. Stir pepper jelly and soy sauce into broth in skillet; cook over medium heat until jelly melts, stirring often.

4. Combine water, cornstarch, and salt, stirring with a wire whisk until smooth. Stir cornstarch mixture into broth mixture; cook over medium heat, stirring constantly, until thickened and bubbly. Return chicken to skillet; cook until thoroughly heated.

5. Combine rice and green onions. Place ½ cup rice mixture on each individual serving plate. Top evenly with chicken tenders and sauce. Sprinkle with toasted sesame seeds. Yield: 4 servings.

Turkey Quesadillas *(photo, page 117)*

TIME: PREP 15 MINUTES; COOK 7 MINUTES

1	teaspoon vegetable oil
1½	cups chopped green pepper
1	cup minced purple onion
2	teaspoons ground cumin
2	cups chopped cooked turkey breast
1	(14½-ounce) can no-salt-added diced tomatoes, drained
¼	cup minced fresh cilantro
¼	teaspoon salt
¼	teaspoon ground black pepper
8	(8-inch) fat-free flour tortillas
¾	cup (3 ounces) shredded reduced-fat Monterey Jack cheese

Butter-flavored vegetable cooking spray
Fresh cilantro sprigs (optional)

SELECTIONS

1 PROTEIN/MILK

1 BREAD

1 FRUIT/VEGETABLE

70 BONUS CALORIES

POINTS

4

PER SERVING

205 CALORIES

29.8G CARBOHYDRATE

3.5G FAT (1.5G SATURATED)

2.3G FIBER

12.5G PROTEIN

20MG CHOLESTEROL

648MG SODIUM

115MG CALCIUM

1.9MG IRON

1. Place oil in a large nonstick skillet over medium-high heat until hot. Add chopped pepper and onion; cook 3 minutes, stirring often. Add cumin, and cook 1 minute, stirring often. Add turkey and tomato; cook 3 minutes, stirring often. Stir in minced cilantro, salt, and ground pepper.

2. Place about ½ cup turkey mixture on half of each tortilla. Sprinkle cheese evenly over turkey mixture on tortillas; fold tortillas in half. Coat a large nonstick skillet with cooking spray; place over medium-high heat until hot. Add 2 filled tortillas; cook 30 seconds on each side or until lightly browned. Set aside, and keep warm. Repeat procedure with remaining 6 tortillas. Garnish with cilantro sprigs, if desired. Serve immediately. Yield: 8 servings.

For crispier quesadillas, bake the filled tortillas at 375° for 8 minutes or until lightly browned instead of browning them in a skillet.

Turkey Vegetable Pie

TIME: PREP 19 MINUTES; COOK 42 MINUTES

SELECTIONS

1 PROTEIN/MILK

1 BREAD

1 FRUIT/VEGETABLE

1 FAT

60 BONUS CALORIES

POINTS

5

PER SERVING

236 CALORIES

25.9G CARBOHYDRATE

6.1G FAT (1.2G SATURATED)

2.4G FIBER

19.2G PROTEIN

30MG CHOLESTEROL

462MG SODIUM

94MG CALCIUM

2.6MG IRON

Vegetable cooking spray

1	tablespoon reduced-calorie margarine
1½	cups sliced fresh mushrooms
1½	cups broccoli flowerets
½	cup sliced carrot
½	cup chopped green onions
1½	tablespoons all-purpose flour
2	teaspoons dry mustard
¼	teaspoon dried thyme
1	(10½-ounce) can low-sodium chicken broth
1½	cups chopped cooked turkey breast (skinned before cooking and cooked without salt)
¾	cup reduced-fat biscuit and baking mix
1	egg white, beaten
½	cup skim milk
2	teaspoons Dijon mustard

No need to make a crust for this pie; biscuit mix batter poured over the turkey and vegetables bakes into a thick crustless filling.

1. Coat a nonstick skillet with cooking spray; add margarine. Place over medium-high heat until margarine melts. Add mushrooms and next 3 ingredients; cook 5 minutes or until vegetables are tender, stirring often. Stir flour, dry mustard, and thyme into broth; add to vegetable mixture. Cook, stirring constantly, 2 to 3 minutes or until mixture is bubbly; stir in turkey. Spoon mixture into a 9-inch pieplate coated with cooking spray.

2. Place baking mix in a medium bowl. Combine egg white, skim milk, and Dijon mustard; add to baking mix, stirring just until baking mix is moistened. Pour over turkey mixture. Bake at 350° for 35 minutes or until golden. Serve immediately. Yield: 4 servings.

Turkey Kielbasa with Beans and Tomatoes

TIME: PREP 10 MINUTES; COOK 21 MINUTES

1½ cups rigatoni (tubular pasta), uncooked
Vegetable cooking spray
10 ounces turkey kielbasa, cut into ½-inch slices
1½ cups chopped onion
4 cloves garlic, minced
1 (16-ounce) can cannellini beans, drained
1 (14½-ounce) can no-salt-added diced tomatoes, undrained
2 tablespoons balsamic vinegar
1 teaspoon dried thyme
¼ teaspoon salt
½ teaspoon ground pepper

SELECTIONS

2 PROTEIN/MILK

2 BREAD

1 FRUIT/VEGETABLE

60 BONUS CALORIES

POINTS

6

PER SERVING

362 CALORIES

54.3G CARBOHYDRATE

6.7G FAT (1.9G SATURATED)

8.1G FIBER

21.7G PROTEIN

44MG CHOLESTEROL

979MG SODIUM

71MG CALCIUM

4.2MG IRON

1. Cook pasta according to package directions, omitting salt and fat; drain and keep warm.

2. Coat a large nonstick skillet with cooking spray; place over medium heat until hot. Add sausage and onion; cook 8 minutes, stirring often. Add garlic; cook 1 minute, stirring often. Stir in beans and remaining 5 ingredients. Bring to a boil; cover, reduce heat, and simmer 10 minutes. Stir in pasta. Serve immediately. Yield: 4 servings.

Spicy turkey kielbasa gives this one-dish meal lots of flavor. If you can't find kielbasa, substitute sweet Italian turkey sausage or even turkey breakfast links.

Penne with Sausage, Peppers, and Tomatoes

TIME: PREP 5 MINUTES; COOK 13 MINUTES

SELECTIONS

1 PROTEIN/MILK

2 BREAD

1 FRUIT/VEGETABLE

40 BONUS CALORIES

POINTS

6

PER SERVING

308 CALORIES

39.9G CARBOHYDRATE

7.7G FAT (2.7G SATURATED)

2.3G FIBER

19.1G PROTEIN

52MG CHOLESTEROL

448MG SODIUM

121MG CALCIUM

2.9MG IRON

6   ounces penne (tubular pasta), uncooked

Vegetable cooking spray

8   ounces sweet Italian turkey sausage, cut into ½-inch slices
     (about 2 sausages)

3   cloves garlic, minced

1   (14½-ounce) can no-salt-added whole tomatoes, undrained
     and chopped

1   (7-ounce) jar roasted sweet red peppers, drained and diced

½   teaspoon ground black pepper

¼   cup grated Parmesan cheese

1. Cook pasta according to package directions, omitting salt and fat; drain and keep warm. Coat a large nonstick skillet with cooking spray; place over medium heat until hot. Add sausage, and cook 8 to 10 minutes or until browned, stirring often; drain well. Set sausage aside. Wipe drippings from skillet with a paper towel.

2. Coat skillet with cooking spray; add garlic, and cook, stirring constantly, 1 minute. Add sausage and tomato. Bring to a boil; reduce heat, and simmer until most of liquid is evaporated. Stir in roasted pepper and ground pepper. Remove from heat.

3. Place pasta in a large bowl; add sausage mixture, and toss. Spoon evenly onto serving plates; sprinkle each serving with 1 tablespoon cheese. Yield: 4 servings.

The easiest way to chop whole canned tomatoes is with kitchen shears while the tomatoes are still in the can.

Sausage-Rice Skillet

TIME: PREP 5 MINUTES; COOK 29 MINUTES

Vegetable cooking spray
6 ounces turkey breakfast sausage, casings removed
1 teaspoon olive oil
1 cup chopped onion
3 cloves garlic, minced
1 small zucchini, sliced
¼ pound fresh green beans, cut into 1-inch pieces
1 (16-ounce) can reduced-sodium chicken broth
½ teaspoon ground red pepper
1 cup long-grain rice, uncooked

1. Coat a large nonstick skillet with cooking spray; place over medium heat until hot. Add sausage, and cook until browned, stirring until it crumbles. Drain and pat dry with paper towels. Set sausage aside. Wipe drippings from skillet with a paper towel.

2. Add oil to skillet; place over medium heat until hot. Add onion, garlic, zucchini, and green beans; cook 5 minutes or until vegetables are tender. Return sausage to skillet; add broth and red pepper. Bring to a boil. Stir in rice; cover, reduce heat, and simmer 20 minutes or until liquid is absorbed and rice is tender. Yield: 4 servings.

Turkey breakfast sausage often is sold frozen, so check the frozen food aisles if it isn't near the pork sausage section of your supermarket. If you buy the sausage in links, rather than in bulk, use kitchen shears to clip the membranes so you can remove the sausage easily.

SELECTIONS

1 PROTEIN/MILK

2 BREAD

1 FRUIT/VEGETABLE

POINTS

6

PER SERVING

287 CALORIES

45.4G CARBOHYDRATE

6.6G FAT (1.7G SATURATED)

1.9G FIBER

12.0G PROTEIN

28MG CHOLESTEROL

264MG SODIUM

56MG CALCIUM

3.5MG IRON

Sausage Hash Brown Frittata

TIME: PREP 12 MINUTES; COOK 18 MINUTES

SELECTIONS

2 PROTEIN/MILK

30 BONUS CALORIES

POINTS

3

PER SERVING

141 CALORIES

11.2G CARBOHYDRATE

4.6G FAT (1.9G SATURATED)

0.4G FIBER

13.6G PROTEIN

25MG CHOLESTEROL

327MG SODIUM

122MG CALCIUM

1.8MG IRON

Vegetable cooking spray

6   ounces turkey breakfast sausage, casings removed

¼   cup sliced green onions

¼   cup chopped sweet red pepper

2   cups frozen country-style hash brown potatoes, thawed

1½   cups fat-free egg substitute

1   tablespoon low-fat ranch-style salad dressing mix

½   cup (2 ounces) shredded reduced-fat sharp Cheddar cheese

1. Coat a large nonstick skillet with cooking spray; place over medium heat until hot. Add sausage, and cook until browned, stirring until it crumbles. Drain and pat dry with paper towels. Set sausage aside. Wipe drippings from skillet with a paper towel.

2. Coat skillet with cooking spray; place over medium-high heat until hot. Add green onions, pepper, and potato; cook, stirring constantly, 5 minutes or until green onions are tender. Add cooked sausage; stir well. Combine egg substitute and dressing mix; pour over vegetable mixture in skillet.

3. Cover and cook over medium-low heat 12 to 13 minutes or until set. Sprinkle with cheese. Cover and cook 2 minutes or until cheese melts. Cut into 6 wedges, and serve immediately. Yield: 6 servings.

If you like omelets, you'll love frittatas. They're easier to make because all the ingredients are stirred in the eggs and cooked together. Turkey sausage, cheese, hash brown potatoes, and sweet red pepper make this version a great breakfast, brunch, or supper treat.

salads

Provençal Tomato Bread Salad *(photo, page 2)*

TIME: PREP 20 MINUTES; CHILL 30 MINUTES

SELECTIONS

1 PROTEIN/MILK
1 BREAD
1 FRUIT/VEGETABLE
1 FAT

POINTS

4

PER SERVING

204 CALORIES
24.4G CARBOHYDRATE
7.4G FAT (3.1G SATURATED)
2.3G FIBER
10.0G PROTEIN
15MG CHOLESTEROL
477MG SODIUM
192MG CALCIUM
1.5MG IRON

8	ounces stale French bread, torn into bite-size pieces
6	ounces part-skim mozzarella cheese, cut into ½-inch cubes
3	medium tomatoes, chopped
1	cup chopped cucumber (about 1 small)
½	cup chopped fresh basil
⅓	cup very thin slices purple onion, cut in half
⅓	cup sliced ripe olives
¼	cup tomato juice
2	tablespoons balsamic vinegar
1	tablespoon olive oil
½	teaspoon ground pepper
¼	teaspoon salt
2	large cloves garlic, minced

Fresh basil sprig (optional)

1. Combine first 7 ingredients in a large bowl; toss gently.

2. Combine tomato juice and next 5 ingredients in a small jar; cover tightly, and shake vigorously. Pour over bread mixture, and toss gently. Cover and chill 30 minutes before serving. Garnish with basil sprig, if desired. Yield: 7 servings.

Stale, dry bread is best for this salad that showcases southern France's finest flavors. It soaks up the dressing as the salad chills. If you don't have stale bread on hand, leave some fresh bread unwrapped on the kitchen counter overnight.

Warm Beef Salad
with Figs
(recipe, page 147)

Corn Salad
(*recipe, page 141*)

Smoked Turkey
Mango Salad
(recipe, page 146)

Beans and Greens Salad *(photo, opposite page)*

TIME: PREP 15 MINUTES

1 (5-ounce) package mixed baby salad greens
1 (16-ounce) can red kidney beans, drained
1 (15-ounce) can cannellini beans, drained
1 medium onion, cut in half lengthwise and thinly sliced
      crosswise
¼ cup chopped fresh basil
2 tablespoons fresh lemon juice
1 tablespoon white wine vinegar
1 tablespoon olive oil
1 tablespoon prepared mustard
½ teaspoon ground pepper
¼ teaspoon salt

SELECTIONS

1 BREAD

1 FRUIT/VEGETABLE

1 FAT

POINTS

4

PER SERVING

203 CALORIES

31.3G CARBOHYDRATE

4.2G FAT (0.6G SATURATED)

3.5G FIBER

10.6G PROTEIN

0MG CHOLESTEROL

338MG SODIUM

67MG CALCIUM

3.6MG IRON

1. Combine first 5 ingredients in a large bowl; toss gently.

2. Combine lemon juice and remaining 5 ingredients in a jar; cover tightly, and shake vigorously. Pour over salad, and toss gently. Yield: 4 servings.

If you can't find the convenient package of mixed baby salad greens, use a 4-cup mixture of salad greens like escarole, radicchio, endive, and romaine lettuce.

Mexican Napa Slaw

TIME: PREP 20 MINUTES; CHILL 1 HOUR

SELECTIONS
1 FRUIT/VEGETABLE
30 BONUS CALORIES

POINTS
1

PER SERVING
49 CALORIES
7.7G CARBOHYDRATE
2.0G FAT (0.3G SATURATED)
1.2G FIBER
1.5G PROTEIN
0MG CHOLESTEROL
110MG SODIUM
65MG CALCIUM
1.0MG IRON

6 cups shredded napa cabbage
2 cups alfalfa sprouts
¾ cup peeled and very thinly sliced jicama
¼ cup chopped fresh cilantro
1 medium-size sweet red pepper, slivered
1 Anaheim chile pepper, seeded and minced
2 green onions, finely chopped
2 tablespoons fresh lime juice
1 tablespoon olive oil
2 tablespoons sugar
½ teaspoon ground black pepper
¼ teaspoon salt
2 cloves garlic, crushed

1. Combine first 7 ingredients in a large bowl. Combine lime juice and remaining 5 ingredients in a small bowl; add to vegetables, and toss well. Cover and chill 1 hour, stirring occasionally. Yield: 8 servings.

Jicama (HEE-ka-ma) is an ugly brown-skinned vegetable with a crisp, white flesh similar to a turnip. It takes on the flavor of other ingredients and adds a crunchy texture.

Corn Salad *(photo, page 136)*

TIME: PREP 15 MINUTES; COOK 1 MINUTE; CHILL 1 HOUR

4	cups fresh or frozen whole-kernel corn
1	cup chopped green pepper
½	cup chopped purple onion
¼	cup chopped fresh parsley
¼	cup balsamic vinegar
1	tablespoon plus 1 teaspoon honey mustard
2	teaspoons olive oil
½	teaspoon salt
½	teaspoon ground black pepper

SELECTIONS

1 BREAD

POINTS

1

PER SERVING

76 CALORIES

14.8G CARBOHYDRATE

2.1G FAT (0.3G SATURATED)

2.4G FIBER

2.2G PROTEIN

0MG CHOLESTEROL

164MG SODIUM

5MG CALCIUM

0.6MG IRON

1. Cook corn in boiling water 1 minute; drain. Combine corn, green pepper, onion, and parsley in a large bowl.

2. Combine vinegar and remaining 4 ingredients in a jar; cover tightly, and shake vigorously. Pour over corn mixture, and toss gently. Cover and chill 1 hour. Yield: 10 servings.

To find out if fresh ears of corn are at their sweetest, pop open a kernel with your fingernail. If the juice is milky white, rather than clear, the corn is at its sweetest.

Vegetable-Couscous Salad with Citrus Vinaigrette

TIME: PREP 15 MINUTES; COOK 5 MINUTES; CHILL 1 HOUR

1¼	cups water
1	cup uncooked couscous
1	cup chopped carrot
1	cup chopped broccoli
1	cup chopped cauliflower
½	cup chopped green onions
¼	cup chopped fresh parsley
1	medium tomato, seeded and chopped
¾	cup unsweetened orange juice
2	tablespoons white wine vinegar
1	tablespoon olive oil
1	tablespoon Dijon mustard

1. Bring water to a boil in a small saucepan; stir in couscous. Cover, remove from heat, and let stand 5 minutes. Transfer couscous to a large bowl. Add carrot and next 5 ingredients; stir well.

2. Combine orange juice and remaining 3 ingredients; stir well. Pour over couscous mixture; toss well. Cover and chill at least 1 hour. Yield: 7 servings.

To seed a tomato, cut it in half horizontally and gently squeeze the seeds from each half. Or scoop the seeds out with a spoon.

Asian-Flavored Pasta Salad

TIME: PREP 15 MINUTES; COOK 10 MINUTES

1   (7-ounce) package spaghetti or 6 ounces Chinese noodles, uncooked

2   cups small fresh broccoli flowerets

¼   cup sliced green onions

1   small sweet red pepper, thinly sliced

2   tablespoons white wine vinegar

2   tablespoons water

2   tablespoons crunchy reduced-fat peanut butter

2   teaspoons peeled, grated gingerroot

¼   teaspoon salt

¼   teaspoon dried crushed red pepper

1. Cook pasta according to package directions, omitting salt and fat. Add broccoli to cooking water 1 minute before pasta is done. Drain pasta and broccoli well; transfer to a large bowl, and add green onions and sweet red pepper. Set aside, and cool slightly.

2. Combine vinegar and remaining 5 ingredients; stir well. Add vinegar mixture to pasta mixture, stirring well. Serve at room temperature. Yield: 5 servings.

> If you mix the vinegar dressing and chop the vegetables while the pasta cooks, you can make this recipe in just **15** minutes.

SELECTIONS

2 BREAD

1 FRUIT/VEGETABLE

30 BONUS CALORIES

POINTS

4

PER SERVING

207 CALORIES

36.8G CARBOHYDRATE

3.3G FAT (0.6G SATURATED)

2.3G FIBER

8.1G PROTEIN

0MG CHOLESTEROL

181MG SODIUM

41MG CALCIUM

2.6MG IRON

Waldorf Salad

TIME: PREP 10 MINUTES

SELECTIONS

1 FRUIT/VEGETABLE

1 FAT

POINTS

2

PER SERVING

84 CALORIES

15.3G CARBOHYDRATE

3.0G FAT (0.4G SATURATED)

2.2G FIBER

0.6G PROTEIN

3MG CHOLESTEROL

95MG SODIUM

16MG CALCIUM

0.3MG IRON

1 (8-ounce) can unsweetened pineapple tidbits, undrained
1 cup unpeeled, chopped golden Delicious apple
1 cup unpeeled, chopped red Delicious apple
1 tablespoon lemon juice
1 cup chopped celery
¼ cup reduced-calorie mayonnaise
3 tablespoons raisins
Lettuce leaves (optional)

1. Drain pineapple, reserving 1 tablespoon juice. Combine apples, reserved pineapple juice, and lemon juice in a medium bowl, tossing to coat apples. Stir in pineapple, celery, mayonnaise, and raisins. Serve immediately or chill at least 1 hour, if desired. Serve on lettuce leaves, if desired. Yield: 6 servings.

Add surprise to a family favorite by using some of the newer apple varieties instead of Delicious apples. Try other sweet, crisp apples like Gala and Fuji.

Curry Chicken Salad

TIME: PREP 20 MINUTES; CHILL 1 HOUR

1½   cups peeled, chopped apple
1   teaspoon lemon juice
3   cups chopped cooked chicken breast
¾   cup thinly sliced celery
¼   cup raisins
⅓   cup low-fat mayonnaise
⅓   cup nonfat sour cream
2   tablespoons minced fresh chives
2   teaspoons sugar
½   teaspoon curry powder
¼   teaspoon salt
2   tablespoons slivered almonds, toasted and chopped

SELECTIONS

3 PROTEIN/MILK
1 FRUIT/VEGETABLE

POINTS

4

PER SERVING

220 CALORIES
16.8G CARBOHYDRATE
5.2G FAT (0.9G SATURATED)
1.8G FIBER
25.8G PROTEIN
66MG CHOLESTEROL
301MG SODIUM
45MG CALCIUM
1.2MG IRON

1. Combine apple and lemon juice in a large bowl; toss well to coat apple. Add chicken, celery, and raisins; toss well.

2. Combine mayonnaise and next 5 ingredients in a small bowl; pour over chicken mixture, and toss well. Sprinkle with chopped almonds. Cover and chill at least 1 hour. Yield: 6 servings.

If you don't have 3 cups of leftover chicken, cook 1 pound of boneless, skinless chicken breasts on a baking sheet in the oven at 450° for 12 to 14 minutes or until the juices run clear; the chicken will be juicier than if you simmer it in water. To save time, toast the almonds on the same baking sheet during the last 3 minutes of cooking.

Smoked Turkey Mango Salad *(photo, page 137)*

TIME: PREP 12 MINUTES

SELECTIONS

1 PROTEIN/MILK

2 FRUIT/VEGETABLE

1 FAT

30 BONUS CALORIES

POINTS

3

PER SERVING

135 CALORIES

14.2G CARBOHYDRATE

4.6G FAT (1.1G SATURATED)

1.7G FIBER

11.5G PROTEIN

24MG CHOLESTEROL

491MG SODIUM

36MG CALCIUM

1.1MG IRON

6	ounces smoked turkey breast, cut into very thin strips
4	cups thinly sliced savoy cabbage
1	cup finely chopped mango
½	cup chopped fresh cilantro
½	medium-size purple onion, slivered
3	tablespoons unsweetened grapefruit juice
2	tablespoons cider vinegar
1	tablespoon olive oil
½	teaspoon ground pepper
¼	teaspoon salt

1. Combine first 5 ingredients in a large bowl. Combine grapefruit juice and remaining 4 ingredients in a small jar; cover tightly, and shake vigorously. Pour dressing over salad, and toss gently. Serve immediately. Yield: 4 servings.

Mangoes are ripe and sweet when they're as soft as a ripe banana. The grapefruit-vinegar dressing provides a delicious flavor contrast to the sweet fruit.

Warm Beef Salad with Figs *(photo, page 135)*

TIME: PREP 14 MINUTES; MARINATE 8 HOURS; COOK 13 MINUTES

2   tablespoons dry red wine

1   tablespoon minced fresh oregano

1   tablespoon minced fresh rosemary

1   tablespoon minced fresh marjoram

1   tablespoon minced fresh thyme

2   teaspoons olive oil

2   large cloves garlic, minced

12 ounces lean boneless beef round steak (¾ inch thick)

¼   cup plain nonfat yogurt

2   tablespoons white wine vinegar

2   tablespoons honey mustard

2   tablespoons unsweetened orange juice

Vegetable cooking spray

4   cups mixed baby salad greens

1   cup snow pea pods, trimmed and cut into very thin strips

8   large fresh or dried figs, sliced

SELECTIONS

2 PROTEIN/MILK

3 FRUIT/VEGETABLE

1 FAT

70 BONUS CALORIES

POINTS

5

PER SERVING

259 CALORIES

22.5G CARBOHYDRATE

8.5G FAT (1.8G SATURATED)

5.4G FIBER

23.4G PROTEIN

55MG CHOLESTEROL

125MG SODIUM

97MG CALCIUM

3.5MG IRON

1. Combine first 7 ingredients; rub herb mixture over both sides of steak. Place steak in a heavy-duty, zip-top plastic bag; seal bag. Marinate in refrigerator 8 hours.

2. Combine yogurt, vinegar, mustard, and orange juice in a small bowl; stir well, and set aside.

3. Place steak on rack of a broiler pan coated with cooking spray. Broil 5½ inches from heat (with electric oven door partially opened) 3 to 4 minutes on each side or to desired degree of doneness. Let stand 5 minutes; cut into thin strips. Arrange lettuce, snow peas, and figs on a serving platter; arrange steak evenly over lettuce. Stir dressing, and drizzle over salad. Yield: 4 servings.

In late summer when figs are ripe, use the fresh ones. But this salad also is delicious with dried figs.

Tuna-Potato Salad

TIME: PREP 15 MINUTES; COOK 25 MINUTES

SELECTIONS

1 PROTEIN/MILK
1 BREAD
2 FRUIT/VEGETABLE
1 FAT

POINTS

5

PER SERVING

258 CALORIES
32.4G CARBOHYDRATE
4.7G FAT (0.6G SATURATED)
5.2G FIBER
24.4G PROTEIN
36MG CHOLESTEROL
284MG SODIUM
106MG CALCIUM
2.8MG IRON

1 pound small round red potatoes
1 cup frozen cut green beans
2 (6-ounce) cans 60%-less-salt tuna in water, drained and flaked into large pieces
½ cup plain nonfat yogurt
3 tablespoons reduced-calorie mayonnaise
1 teaspoon Dijon mustard
2 anchovy fillets, rinsed and minced
1 small clove garlic, minced
2 medium tomatoes, thinly sliced
1 medium cucumber, thinly sliced
1 lemon, cut into wedges

1. Cook potatoes in boiling water to cover 25 minutes or until tender; drain and let cool completely. Cut potatoes into ½-inch cubes.

2. Cook green beans in a small amount of boiling water 5 minutes or until crisp-tender. Drain beans, and place in ice water until cool; drain. Combine potato, beans, and tuna in a large bowl.

3. Combine yogurt and next 4 ingredients; add to potato mixture, and toss gently. To serve, spoon tuna mixture in center of a serving plate; arrange tomato, cucumber, and lemon wedges around tuna mixture. Yield: 4 servings.

One-half of a 10-ounce package of frozen green beans equals 1 cup of beans.

side dishes

Asparagus with Cheese Sauce *(photo, page 155)*

TIME: PREP 7 MINUTES; COOK 15 MINUTES

SELECTIONS

30 BONUS CALORIES

POINTS

1

PER SERVING

50 CALORIES

5.2G CARBOHYDRATE

1.8G FAT (0.9G SATURATED)

1.0G FIBER

4.0G PROTEIN

4MG CHOLESTEROL

122MG SODIUM

108MG CALCIUM

0.5MG IRON

3   pounds fresh asparagus spears

2   teaspoons reduced-calorie margarine

1   tablespoon all-purpose flour

1   cup evaporated skimmed milk

½   cup (2 ounces) finely shredded provolone cheese

¼   teaspoon salt

Paprika (optional)

1. Snap off tough ends of asparagus. Remove scales with a vegetable peeler, if desired. Arrange asparagus in a steamer basket over boiling water; cover and steam 6 to 8 minutes or until crisp-tender.

2. Melt margarine in a small heavy saucepan over medium heat; add flour. Cook, stirring constantly with a wire whisk, 1 minute. Gradually add milk, stirring constantly until mixture is thickened and bubbly. Add cheese and salt, stirring until cheese melts. Arrange asparagus on a serving platter; pour cheese sauce over asparagus. Sprinkle with paprika, if desired. Serve warm. Yield: 12 servings.

> For the most succulent asparagus, look for the thinnest, most delicate spears.

Molasses Beans with Ham

1	teaspoon vegetable oil
2	cups chopped onion
½	cup chopped lean cooked ham
2	(15-ounce) cans red kidney beans, drained
1	cup canned no-salt-added beef broth, undiluted and divided
2	tablespoons molasses
2	teaspoons Dijon mustard
2	teaspoons cornstarch
½	teaspoon ground pepper

SELECTIONS

1 PROTEIN/MILK

1 BREAD

POINTS

2

PER SERVING

125 CALORIES

21.5G CARBOHYDRATE

1.3G FAT (0.3G SATURATED)

2.8G FIBER

7.2G PROTEIN

4MG CHOLESTEROL

260MG SODIUM

36MG CALCIUM

2.1MG IRON

1. Heat oil in a large nonstick skillet over medium-high heat until hot. Add onion, and cook 7 minutes or until tender, stirring often. Add ham, and cook 2 minutes, stirring often.

2. Add beans, ¾ cup plus 2 tablespoons broth, molasses, and mustard to onion mixture. Bring to a boil; reduce heat, and simmer, uncovered, 20 minutes.

3. Combine remaining 2 tablespoons broth and cornstarch in a small bowl; stir well. Add to bean mixture. Cook, stirring constantly, 1 minute or until thickened and bubbly. Stir in pepper. Yield: 8 servings.

Molasses adds a wonderfully strong and distinctive sweet flavor, but you can substitute honey or maple syrup instead.

Lemon-Marinated Vegetables

TIME: PREP 10 MINUTES; COOK 4 MINUTES; MARINATE 2 HOURS

SELECTIONS

2 FRUIT/VEGETABLE

POINTS

1

PER SERVING

62 CALORIES

10.7G CARBOHYDRATE

1.1G FAT (0.2G SATURATED)

3.4G FIBER

4.0G PROTEIN

0MG CHOLESTEROL

82MG SODIUM

58MG CALCIUM

1.2MG IRON

2   medium carrots, scraped and thinly sliced
1   cup water
4   cups broccoli flowerets
2   cups shredded red cabbage
1   cup frozen English peas, thawed
2   teaspoons grated lemon rind
2   tablespoons fresh lemon juice
2   tablespoons rice wine vinegar
1   teaspoon reduced-sodium soy sauce
1   teaspoon olive oil
2   cloves garlic, minced
¼   teaspoon ground pepper

1. Place carrot in a large saucepan. Add water to carrot, and bring to a boil; cover and cook 2 minutes. Add broccoli to carrot; cover and cook 2 minutes. Drain vegetables, and rinse with cold water; transfer to a large bowl. Add cabbage and peas to carrot mixture, tossing to combine. Set aside.

2. Combine lemon rind and remaining 6 ingredients in a small bowl; stir with a wire whisk until well blended. Pour vinaigrette over vegetables, and toss to coat. Cover and chill 2 hours, stirring occasionally. Yield: 6 servings.

The predominant lemon flavor is at its best after just a few hours of chilling. Don't try to make this the day before you serve it or the lemony vinaigrette flavor may be too strong and the acid from the lemon juice may discolor some of the vegetables.

Balsamic Carrots

TIME: PREP 7 MINUTES; COOK 12 MINUTES

1	pound carrots (about 5 small), scraped and sliced diagonally
1	cup water
2	tablespoons balsamic vinegar
2	teaspoons honey
1	teaspoon olive oil
½	teaspoon Dijon mustard
1	teaspoon dried basil
⅛	teaspoon ground pepper

1. Place carrot in a large saucepan; add water, and bring to a boil. Cover, reduce heat, and simmer 10 minutes or until tender. Drain; return carrot to saucepan.

2. Combine vinegar and remaining 5 ingredients in a small bowl, stirring well with a wire whisk; add to carrot. Cook over medium heat 2 minutes, stirring often. Serve warm. Yield: 4 servings.

The mellow flavor of aged balsamic vinegar is responsible for the unique taste of these carrots. It's a bit more expensive than distilled white or cider vinegar, but it's worth keeping on your pantry shelf.

SELECTIONS

1 FRUIT/VEGETABLE

POINTS

1

PER SERVING

62 CALORIES

12.5G CARBOHYDRATE

1.4G FAT (0.2G SATURATED)

3.0G FIBER

1.0G PROTEIN

0MG CHOLESTEROL

51MG SODIUM

31MG CALCIUM

0.7MG IRON

Minted Sugar Snaps *(photo, page 157)*

TIME: PREP 12 MINUTES; COOK 3 MINUTES

SELECTIONS

1 FRUIT/VEGETABLE

POINTS

0

PER SERVING

30 CALORIES

5.2G CARBOHYDRATE

0.4G FAT (0.0G SATURATED)

1.7G FIBER

1.7G PROTEIN

0MG CHOLESTEROL

97MG SODIUM

32MG CALCIUM

1.4MG IRON

Vegetable cooking spray

1   (8-ounce) package fresh Sugar Snap peas, trimmed

2   green onions, chopped

1   large clove garlic, minced

2   tablespoons minced fresh mint

⅛   teaspoon salt

¼   teaspoon ground pepper

Fresh mint sprigs (optional)

1. Coat a large nonstick skillet with cooking spray, and place over medium heat until hot. Add peas, green onions, and garlic; cook 3 minutes or until peas are crisp-tender, stirring often. Remove from heat; stir in mint, salt, and pepper. Garnish with mint sprigs, if desired. Yield: 3 servings.

This recipe will work just as well with frozen *Sugar Snap* peas. Thaw them overnight in the refrigerator or defrost in the microwave.

Asparagus with Cheese
Sauce (*recipe, page 150*)

Orange-Scented Couscous
Timbales (*recipe, page 168*)

Minted Sugar Snaps
(recipe, page 154)

Stir-Fried Brown Rice
(recipe, page 170)

Linguine Verde
(recipe, page 167)

Herbed English Peas with Mushrooms

TIME: PREP 3 MINUTES; COOK 12 MINUTES

1	teaspoon vegetable oil
½	cup thinly sliced onion
1½	cups sliced fresh mushrooms
1½	cups frozen English peas, thawed
2	tablespoons water
¼	teaspoon salt
1	teaspoon dried tarragon
⅛	teaspoon ground pepper

1. Heat oil in a large nonstick skillet over medium heat until hot. Add onion; cook 4 minutes or until tender, stirring often. Add mushrooms; cook 4 minutes or until tender, stirring often. Stir in peas and remaining ingredients; cover and cook 4 minutes or just until peas are tender. Serve immediately. Yield: 4 servings.

If you don't have tarragon, use the same amount of any savory herb like oregano or basil. If fresh herbs are in season, substitute 1 tablespoon of a minced fresh herb for each teaspoon of any dried herb.

SELECTIONS

1 BREAD

1 FRUIT/VEGETABLE

POINTS

1

PER SERVING

69 CALORIES

10.0G CARBOHYDRATE

1.3G FAT (0.2G SATURATED)

2.5G FIBER

3.6G PROTEIN

0MG CHOLESTEROL

212MG SODIUM

17MG CALCIUM

1.3MG IRON

Marinated Mushrooms

TIME: PREP 12 MINUTES; MARINATE 8 HOURS

SELECTIONS

1 FRUIT/VEGETABLE
40 BONUS CALORIES

POINTS

1

PER SERVING

50 CALORIES
11.0G CARBOHYDRATE
0.2G FAT (0.0G SATURATED)
0.8G FIBER
1.1G PROTEIN
0MG CHOLESTEROL
392MG SODIUM
11MG CALCIUM
1.1MG IRON

1	pound small whole fresh mushrooms
1	cup fat-free balsamic vinaigrette
¼	cup chopped fresh chives
1	tablespoon minced fresh thyme
1	clove garlic, minced
½	teaspoon sugar
¼	teaspoon ground pepper

1. Combine all ingredients in a large heavy-duty, zip-top plastic bag; seal bag, and shake well. Marinate in refrigerator 8 hours, turning bag occasionally. Serve with a slotted spoon. Yield: 8 servings.

To reduce the marinating time to 2 hours, cut each mushroom in half lengthwise. The cut sides will absorb marinade flavors more quickly.

Hash Brown Casserole

TIME: PREP 5 MINUTES; COOK 30 MINUTES

1   (10¾-ounce) can reduced-fat, reduced-sodium cream of
        mushroom soup, undiluted
½   cup low-fat sour cream
½   cup (2 ounces) shredded reduced-fat sharp Cheddar cheese
¼   cup chopped green onions
¼   cup skim milk
⅛   teaspoon ground red pepper
⅛   teaspoon ground nutmeg (optional)
½   (32-ounce) package frozen hash brown potatoes
Butter-flavored vegetable cooking spray
½   cup crushed corn flakes cereal

1. Combine first 6 ingredients in a large bowl, stirring well. Stir in
nutmeg, if desired. Stir in hash brown potatoes; pour into an 11- x 7-
x 1½-inch baking dish coated with cooking spray. Sprinkle with
crushed corn flakes; coat cornflakes with cooking spray. Bake at 350°
for 30 minutes or until bubbly. Serve immediately. Yield: 8 servings.

> To get ½ cup of crushed corn flakes cereal, measure 1⅓
> cups corn flakes cereal into a heavy duty, zip-top plastic bag. Seal
> the bag, and crush the flakes with your hands or a rolling pin. It's a
> great job for kids who like to help in the kitchen.

SELECTIONS

1 BREAD

30 BONUS CALORIES

POINTS

3

PER SERVING

116 CALORIES

15.6G CARBOHYDRATE

4.2G FAT (2.2G SATURATED)

0.6G FIBER

4.6G PROTEIN

14MG CHOLESTEROL

234MG SODIUM

100MG CALCIUM

0.5MG IRON

Italian-Style Potatoes and Green Beans

TIME: PREP 8 MINUTES; COOK 22 MINUTES

½   pound small round red potatoes, unpeeled

1   (9-ounce) package frozen cut green beans, thawed

1   teaspoon olive oil

1   clove garlic, minced

1   (14½-ounce) can Italian-style stewed tomatoes, undrained

2   teaspoons minced fresh oregano

¼   teaspoon salt

1. Place potatoes in a large saucepan; add water to cover, and bring to a boil. Cover and cook 10 minutes. Add green beans, and cook 5 to 7 minutes or until beans and potatoes are tender. Drain well; slice potatoes.

2. Heat oil in a large skillet over medium-high heat until hot. Add garlic; cook 1 minute, stirring often. Add tomato, oregano, and salt; bring to a boil. Reduce heat, and simmer 5 minutes. Stir in potato and beans, and cook until vegetables are thoroughly heated. Serve with a slotted spoon. Yield: 4 servings.

For an easy menu, serve this vegetable combo with grilled boneless chicken breast halves and French rolls.

Spiced Stuffed Sweet Potatoes

4	small sweet potatoes (about 2 pounds)
¼	cup nonfat cream cheese
¼	teaspoon salt
½	teaspoon ground cinnamon
⅛	teaspoon ground allspice
⅛	teaspoon ground nutmeg
3	tablespoons raisins

SELECTIONS

1 BREAD

POINTS

2

PER SERVING

159 CALORIES

35.1G CARBOHYDRATE

0.4G FAT (0.1G SATURATED)

4.0G FIBER

4.2G PROTEIN

3MG CHOLESTEROL

248MG SODIUM

74MG CALCIUM

0.9MG IRON

1. Scrub sweet potatoes. Bake at 450° for 1 hour or until tender; let cool slightly. Cut a lengthwise strip from top of each potato; discard strips. Scoop out pulp, leaving ¼-inch-thick shells; set shells aside.

2. Place potato pulp in a medium bowl; add cream cheese and next 4 ingredients. Beat at medium speed of an electric mixer until fluffy. Stir in raisins. Spoon mixture evenly into sweet potato shells; place on an ungreased baking sheet. Bake at 400° for 10 minutes or until thoroughly heated. Yield: 4 servings.

You'll cut 40 minutes off the cooking time if you cook the sweet potatoes in the microwave. Pierce the potatoes with a fork in several places, and then arrange in a circle on a paper towel. Microwave at HIGH 12 to 14 minutes, rearranging the potatoes after 5 minutes. Allow them to stand at least 5 minutes.

Grilled Tomatoes

TIME: PREP 6 MINUTES; COOK 15 MINUTES

SELECTIONS

1 FRUIT/VEGETABLE

POINTS

1

PER SERVING

46 CALORIES

6.8G CARBOHYDRATE

1.7G FAT (0.2G SATURATED)

1.0G FIBER

1.3G PROTEIN

0MG CHOLESTEROL

217MG SODIUM

19MG CALCIUM

0.6MG IRON

2   large firm ripe tomatoes

3   tablespoons fine, dry breadcrumbs

2   tablespoons minced fresh basil

1   tablespoon minced fresh parsley

1   tablespoon rinsed and drained capers, minced

1   large clove garlic, minced

1   teaspoon olive oil

Vegetable cooking spray

1. Cut tomatoes in half horizontally. Scoop out seeds with the tip of a spoon, leaving pulp intact; discard seeds. Set tomato halves aside.

2. Combine breadcrumbs and next 4 ingredients in a bowl. Spoon breadcrumb mixture evenly into tomato halves. Drizzle with oil.

3. Coat grill rack with cooking spray; place on grill over medium-hot coals (350° to 400°). Tear off a 12-inch square piece of aluminum foil; poke holes in foil with a wooden pick. Place foil on grill; arrange tomato halves on foil. Grill, covered, 15 minutes or until tomato halves are tender. Yield: 4 servings.

You can broil these tomato halves instead of grilling them: Broil them 5½ inches from heat (with electric oven door partially opened) 6 minutes or to desired degree of doneness.

Italian Stuffed Zucchini

TIME: PREP **20** MINUTES; COOK **52** MINUTES

4	large zucchini
¼	teaspoon salt
Vegetable cooking spray	
1	teaspoon olive oil
1	cup finely chopped onion
3	cloves garlic, minced
½	cup finely chopped plum tomato
⅓	cup fine, dry breadcrumbs
¼	cup chopped fresh parsley
3	tablespoons grated Parmesan cheese
1	tablespoon pine nuts, toasted
½	teaspoon ground pepper

SELECTIONS

1 FRUIT/VEGETABLE

40 BONUS CALORIES

POINTS

1

PER SERVING

69 CALORIES

9.4G CARBOHYDRATE

2.6G FAT (0.8G SATURATED)

1.4G FIBER

3.6G PROTEIN

2MG CHOLESTEROL

164MG SODIUM

70MG CALCIUM

1.1MG IRON

1. Cut zucchini in half lengthwise; scoop out pulp, leaving ¼-inch-thick shells. Sprinkle shells with salt; set aside. Coarsely chop pulp.

2. Coat a medium nonstick skillet with cooking spray, and add oil; place over medium-high heat until hot. Add chopped zucchini and onion; cook 10 minutes or until vegetables are tender, stirring occasionally. Add garlic and tomato; cook 2 minutes or until thickened, stirring occasionally. Remove from heat; stir in breadcrumbs and remaining 4 ingredients.

3. Spoon vegetable mixture evenly into zucchini shells. Place in a 13- x 9- x 2-inch baking dish coated with cooking spray. Cover and bake at 375° for 20 minutes. Uncover and bake 20 additional minutes or until zucchini shells are fork-tender and stuffing is lightly browned. Yield: 8 servings.

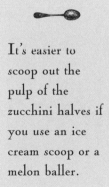

It's easier to scoop out the pulp of the zucchini halves if you use an ice cream scoop or a melon baller.

Fusilli with Mozzarella and Eggplant

TIME: PREP **9** MINUTES; COOK **30** MINUTES

SELECTIONS

1 BREAD

1 FRUIT/VEGETABLE

50 BONUS CALORIES

POINTS

3

PER SERVING

165 CALORIES

28.5G CARBOHYDRATE

2.5G FAT (1.3G SATURATED)

2.0G FIBER

7.8G PROTEIN

7MG CHOLESTEROL

395MG SODIUM

150MG CALCIUM

2.2MG IRON

6   ounces fusilli (corkscrew pasta), uncooked

1   (1-pound) eggplant

1   (14½-ounce) can diced tomatoes with basil, garlic, and oregano, undrained

½   cup chopped celery

½   teaspoon ground pepper

3   ounces part-skim mozzarella cheese, diced

3   tablespoons minced fresh oregano

1. Cook pasta according to package directions, omitting salt and fat; drain well, and keep warm.

2. Peel eggplant, if desired, and cut into 1-inch pieces. Combine eggplant, tomato, celery, and pepper in a large nonstick skillet; bring to a boil. Cover, reduce heat, and simmer 15 minutes. Uncover and simmer 15 additional minutes or until most of liquid evaporates. Remove from heat; stir in pasta. Add cheese and oregano, stirring until cheese melts. Serve immediately. Yield: 7 servings.

> You can substitute other types of pasta for fusilli. Just look for one with a similar shape and size, like elbow macaroni. To save time, let the pasta cook while you prepare the eggplant mixture.

Linguine Verde *(photo, page 158)*

TIME: PREP **8** MINUTES; COOK **10** MINUTES

8	ounces linguine, uncooked	
3	cups loosely packed spinach leaves	
2	cups trimmed watercress	
2	large plum tomatoes, each cut into 8 wedges	
¾	cup loosely packed sliced fresh basil leaves	
2	teaspoons extra-virgin olive oil	
¼	teaspoon salt	
½	cup grated Parmesan cheese	
½	teaspoon ground pepper	

SELECTIONS

1 BREAD

1 FRUIT/VEGETABLE

60 BONUS CALORIES

POINTS

3

PER SERVING

156 CALORIES

23.2G CARBOHYDRATE

3.8G FAT (1.6G SATURATED)

1.6G FIBER

7.3G PROTEIN

6MG CHOLESTEROL

220MG SODIUM

127MG CALCIUM

1.6MG IRON

1. Cook linguine according to package directions, omitting salt and fat. Set aside, and keep warm.

2. Combine spinach and next 5 ingredients in a large bowl; toss well. Add linguine to spinach mixture; sprinkle with Parmesan cheese and pepper, tossing well. Serve immediately. Yield: 8 servings.

> Buy bags of prewashed spinach leaves for the fastest preparation time. (One 10-ounce bag contains 2½ cups torn spinach.) Trim the watercress and cut the tomatoes while the pasta cooks.

Orange-Scented Couscous Timbales *(photo, page 156)*

TIME: PREP 5 MINUTES; COOK 5 MINUTES

<u>SELECTIONS</u>

2 BREAD

<u>POINTS</u>

4

<u>PER SERVING</u>

205 CALORIES

39.0G CARBOHYDRATE

2.8G FAT (0.3G SATURATED)

2.1G FIBER

7.2G PROTEIN

0MG CHOLESTEROL

18MG SODIUM

14MG CALCIUM

1.3MG IRON

1 cup unsweetened orange juice

1 cup canned low-sodium chicken broth, undiluted

1 (10-ounce) package couscous, uncooked

2 teaspoons grated orange rind

Vegetable cooking spray

2 tablespoons sliced almonds, toasted

Orange rind strips (optional)

1. Combine orange juice and chicken broth in a medium saucepan; bring to a boil. Stir in couscous and orange rind; cover and remove from heat. Let stand 5 minutes.

2. Spoon mixture evenly into 6 (6-ounce) custard cups coated with cooking spray. Invert onto a serving platter; sprinkle with almonds. Garnish with orange rind strips, if desired. Yield: 6 servings.

This recipe is the ultimate in ease and speed. If you don't have custard cups for shaping the couscous into timbales, then just fluff it with a fork and serve it as you would rice. To get very fine shavings of orange rind for garnish, use a kitchen tool called a zester.

Walnut-Mushroom Rice

TIME: PREP **5** MINUTES; COOK **28** MINUTES

1	teaspoon olive oil
1	cup chopped onion
1	clove garlic, minced
2	cups sliced fresh mushrooms
2	cups canned low-sodium chicken broth, undiluted
1	cup long-grain rice, uncooked
2	tablespoons chopped walnuts, toasted
2	tablespoons grated Parmesan cheese
2	tablespoons minced fresh parsley
¼	teaspoon salt

SELECTIONS

1 BREAD

POINTS

2

PER SERVING

113 CALORIES

19.0G CARBOHYDRATE

2.6G FAT (0.5G SATURATED)

0.9G FIBER

3.6G PROTEIN

1MG CHOLESTEROL

104MG SODIUM

32MG CALCIUM

1.5MG IRON

1. Heat oil in a large nonstick skillet over medium-high heat until hot. Add onion; cook 3 minutes, stirring often. Add garlic and mushrooms; cook 5 minutes, stirring often. Add broth; bring to a boil. Stir in rice; cover, reduce heat, and simmer 20 to 25 minutes or until broth is absorbed and rice is tender. Stir in walnuts, cheese, parsley, and salt. Serve immediately. Yield: 10 servings.

Toasted walnuts add rich flavor. To toast them quickly, spread the nuts in a 9-inch pieplate, and microwave at HIGH, uncovered, 1 to 3 minutes or until lightly toasted.

Stir-Fried Brown Rice *(photo, page 157)*

TIME: PREP 7 MINUTES; COOK 25 MINUTES

SELECTIONS
1 BREAD
1 FRUIT/VEGETABLE
50 BONUS CALORIES

POINTS
1

PER SERVING
69 CALORIES
13.0G CARBOHYDRATE
1.1G FAT (0.2G SATURATED)
2.1G FIBER
2.5G PROTEIN
0MG CHOLESTEROL
55MG SODIUM
17MG CALCIUM
0.8MG IRON

Vegetable cooking spray
1 teaspoon olive oil
1 cup chopped celery
1 cup thinly sliced carrot
1 cup chopped onion
2 teaspoons ground cumin
2 teaspoons peeled, minced gingerroot
2½ cups canned low-sodium chicken broth, undiluted
⅓ cup dried tomato sprinkles
2 cups instant brown rice, uncooked
2 cups frozen English peas, thawed

1. Coat a large nonstick skillet with cooking spray; add oil, and place over medium-high heat until hot. Add celery, carrot, and onion; cook 4 minutes or until vegetables are tender, stirring often. Stir in cumin and gingerroot; cook, stirring constantly, 1 minute. Add broth, tomato sprinkles, and rice; bring to a boil. Cover, reduce heat, and simmer 15 minutes or until liquid is absorbed and rice is tender. Stir in peas. Yield: 14 servings.

Be sure to use instant brown rice in this recipe; it cooks in less than half the time of regular brown rice.

soups
sandwiches

Minted Strawberry Soup *(photo, page 175)*

TIME: PREP 10 MINUTES

SELECTIONS

1 FRUIT/VEGETABLE

30 BONUS CALORIES

POINTS

1

PER SERVING

61 CALORIES

12.8G CARBOHYDRATE

1.1G FAT (0.7G SATURATED)

0.6G FIBER

0.8G PROTEIN

3MG CHOLESTEROL

5MG SODIUM

24MG CALCIUM

0.6MG IRON

1	(16-ounce) package frozen whole unsweetened strawberries, partially thawed
1¼	cups unsweetened orange juice
2	tablespoons fresh mint leaves
1	tablespoon sugar
¼	cup low-fat sour cream

Strawberry slices (optional)
Fresh mint sprigs (optional)

1. Combine first 4 ingredients in container of an electric blender; cover and process until smooth. Pour into a large bowl; add sour cream, stirring well with a wire whisk. Serve immediately or cover and chill up to 8 hours. To serve, ladle soup into individual bowls. Garnish with strawberry slices and mint sprigs, if desired.
Yield: 7 servings.

🥄 If you partially thaw the berries before you put them in the blender, they'll be easier to blend. And the soup will be cold and ready to serve as an appetizer or as a dessert soup.

Kale and Potato Soup

TIME: PREP 13 MINUTES; COOK 20 MINUTES

2   teaspoons olive oil

1   cup finely chopped onion

4   cloves garlic, minced

¼   teaspoon dried crushed red pepper

6   cups coarsely chopped kale leaves

3   cups peeled, diced round red potato (about 1¼ pounds)

2   (16-ounce) cans low-sodium chicken broth

¼   cup freshly grated Asiago or Parmesan cheese

Ground black pepper

1. Heat oil in a Dutch oven over medium heat until hot. Add onion; cook 5 minutes or until tender, stirring often. Add garlic and red pepper; cook 1 minute, stirring often. Add kale; cook 2 minutes or until wilted, stirring occasionally.

2. Add potato and chicken broth; bring to a boil. Cover, reduce heat, and simmer 20 minutes or until potato is tender. Ladle soup into individual bowls, sprinkle with cheese and black pepper. Yield: 6 servings.

> Be sure to use green kale rather than flowering kale. Green kale works well for this soup if you chop it into thin strips using a long knife with a wide blade like a French or chef's knife.

SELECTIONS

1 BREAD

1 FRUIT/VEGETABLE

POINTS

2

PER SERVING

109 CALORIES

15.1G CARBOHYDRATE

3.6G FAT (1.1G SATURATED)

2.0G FIBER

5.6G PROTEIN

22MG CHOLESTEROL

120MG SODIUM

94MG CALCIUM

4.2MG IRON

Souped-Up Tomato Soup

TIME: PREP 17 MINUTES; COOK 10 MINUTES

SELECTIONS

1 FRUIT/VEGETABLE

30 BONUS CALORIES

POINTS

1

PER SERVING

88 CALORIES

18.2G CARBOHYDRATE

1.9G FAT (0.4G SATURATED)

2.8G FIBER

2.5G PROTEIN

0MG CHOLESTEROL

386MG SODIUM

35MG CALCIUM

0.6MG IRON

1	teaspoon olive oil
1½	cups finely chopped onion (about 2 small)
½	cup finely chopped celery (about 2 stalks)
2	cloves garlic, minced
2	(10¾-ounce) cans reduced-fat, reduced-sodium tomato soup
1	(14½-ounce) can no-salt-added diced tomatoes, undrained
2¾	cups water
¼	cup no-salt-added tomato paste
1	teaspoon dried basil
½	teaspoon ground pepper
¼	teaspoon salt
¼	teaspoon hot sauce

1. Heat oil in a large saucepan over medium-high heat until hot. Add onion, celery, and garlic; cook 7 minutes or until tender, stirring often.

2. Stir in tomato soup and remaining ingredients; bring to a boil, stirring often. Reduce heat, and simmer, uncovered, 10 minutes. Yield: 7 servings.

Start with canned tomato soup, and add onion, celery, garlic, canned tomatoes, and basil. No one will know that you didn't make this soup from scratch.

Minted Strawberry Soup
(recipe, page 172)

Round Italian
Sandwich
(recipe, page 182)

Italian Tortellini Soup

TIME: PREP 14 MINUTES; COOK 30 MINUTES

1	medium fennel bulb
2	teaspoons olive oil
1	cup finely chopped carrot
2	cloves garlic, minced
4	(10½-ounce) cans low-sodium chicken broth
1	bay leaf
¼	teaspoon salt

Ground pepper

1	(9-ounce) package refrigerated cheese-filled tortellini, uncooked
2	cups shredded spinach or escarole
2	tablespoons plus 1 teaspoon grated Romano or Parmesan cheese

1. Trim outer stalks from fennel; cut bulb in half lengthwise, and remove cores. Cut each half vertically into thin slices.

2. Heat oil in a large saucepan over medium heat until hot. Add fennel, carrot, and garlic; cook 10 minutes or until tender, stirring often. Stir in broth and next 3 ingredients. Bring to a boil; cover, reduce heat, and simmer 15 minutes.

3. Stir in pasta and spinach. Bring to a boil; reduce heat, and simmer, uncovered, 5 minutes or until pasta is tender. Remove and discard bay leaf. Ladle soup into individual bowls; sprinkle each serving with 1 teaspoon cheese. Yield: 7 servings.

Escarole is a type of endive with crisp, curly green leaves that taste slightly bitter. The chopped greens will be a bit crisper than spinach in this recipe.

SELECTIONS

1 BREAD

1 FRUIT/VEGETABLE

60 BONUS CALORIES

POINTS

4

PER SERVING

179 CALORIES

22.9G CARBOHYDRATE

5.8G FAT (1.7G SATURATED)

1.3G FIBER

9.2G PROTEIN

19MG CHOLESTEROL

312MG SODIUM

152MG CALCIUM

2.5MG IRON

Turkey Chowder

TIME: PREP 24 MINUTES; COOK 24 MINUTES

SELECTIONS	2 teaspoons reduced-calorie margarine
1 PROTEIN/MILK	¾ pound peeled, diced baking potato
1 BREAD	2 cups chopped onion
30 BONUS CALORIES	1 cup finely chopped celery
	2 (10½-ounce) cans low-sodium chicken broth
POINTS	1 (10-ounce) package frozen whole-kernel corn, thawed
3	1 teaspoon dried thyme
	½ teaspoon salt
PER SERVING	¼ teaspoon pepper
165 CALORIES	2¾ cups chopped cooked turkey breast
21.3G CARBOHYDRATE	1 (12-ounce) can evaporated skimmed milk
1.7G FAT (0.4G SATURATED)	1 tablespoon all-purpose flour
2.1G FIBER	2 tablespoons water
17.2G PROTEIN	
33MG CHOLESTEROL	
240MG SODIUM	
137MG CALCIUM	
1.7MG IRON	

1. Place margarine in a Dutch oven over medium heat until melted. Add potato, onion, and celery to Dutch oven; cook, stirring constantly, 5 minutes. Add broth and next 4 ingredients; bring to a boil. Cover, reduce heat, and simmer 15 minutes.

2. Remove 2 cups vegetables from broth with a slotted spoon; partially mash vegetables with a fork or potato masher. Return vegetables to Dutch oven. Add turkey and milk; bring to a boil over medium heat, stirring constantly. Combine flour and water, stirring until smooth. Gradually add flour mixture to Dutch oven; cook over medium heat, stirring constantly, 4 to 5 minutes or until thickened and bubbly. Yield: 9 servings.

An Idaho or russet baking potato works best for chowder because, when cooked, it mashes easily and makes the broth thick and creamy.

Cioppino

TIME: PREP 15 MINUTES; COOK 20 MINUTES

2	(14½-ounce) cans no-salt-added diced tomatoes, undrained
1	cup reduced-sodium vegetable juice
½	cup clam juice
½	cup water
½	cup chopped green pepper
3	cloves garlic, minced
1	teaspoon dried Italian seasoning
½	teaspoon ground black pepper
¼	teaspoon salt
6	ounces tilapia or other firm white fish fillets, cut into 2-inch pieces
6	ounces red snapper fillets, skinned and cut into 2-inch pieces
½	cup chopped fresh parsley
⅓	cup freshly grated Parmesan cheese

SELECTIONS

1 PROTEIN/MILK

1 FRUIT/VEGETABLE

POINTS

2

PER SERVING

109 CALORIES

9.1G CARBOHYDRATE

2.4G FAT (1.1G SATURATED)

2.6G FIBER

12.9G PROTEIN

30MG CHOLESTEROL

315MG SODIUM

115MG CALCIUM

1.1MG IRON

1. Combine first 9 ingredients in a large saucepan. Bring to a boil; cover, reduce heat, and simmer 10 minutes. Add fish and parsley. Bring to a boil; reduce heat, and simmer, uncovered, 10 minutes or until fish flakes easily when tested with a fork.

2. Ladle soup into individual bowls; sprinkle evenly with cheese. Yield: 7 servings.

Cioppino (chuh PEE noh) is a tomato-flavored fish stew with an Italian accent. Traditionally, this stew features several types of fish, but you can use ¾ pound of any one type, if you prefer.

Mushroom Pizza Melts

TIME: PREP 10 MINUTES; COOK 5 MINUTES

SELECTIONS

1 PROTEIN/MILK

1 BREAD

1 FRUIT/VEGETABLE

POINTS

3

PER SERVING

162 CALORIES

21.6G CARBOHYDRATE

4.6G FAT (2.3G SATURATED)

1.0G FIBER

8.6G PROTEIN

12MG CHOLESTEROL

305MG SODIUM

196MG CALCIUM

1.5MG IRON

Vegetable cooking spray

1	medium-size green pepper
1	cup sliced fresh mushrooms
1	small onion, thinly sliced
2	English muffins, split and lightly toasted
¼	cup pizza sauce
¾	cup (3 ounces) shredded part-skim mozzarella cheese

1. Coat a large nonstick skillet with cooking spray; place over medium-high heat until hot. Cut green pepper into 4 rings; reserve remaining pepper for another use. Add green pepper rings, mushrooms, and onion to skillet; cook 3 minutes or until crisp-tender, stirring often.

2. Spread cut side of each English muffin half with 1 tablespoon pizza sauce. Arrange mushroom mixture over pizza sauce; sprinkle evenly with cheese. Place on a baking sheet; broil 5½ inches from heat (with electric oven door partially opened) 2 minutes or until cheese melts. Yield: 4 servings.

Personalize these pizza sandwiches with your own vegetable toppings or refrigerator leftovers. Roasted red pepper strips, black beans, broccoli flowerets, or slices of summer squash make good toppers. Presliced white mushrooms are easiest to use, but try some specialty mushrooms like crimini or portobello for extra flavor.

Pan Bagna

TIME: PREP 17 MINUTES; CHILL 8 HOURS

1	(18- x 2½-inch) French baguette
2	medium tomatoes, peeled, seeded, and diced
¾	cup (3 ounces) shredded part-skim mozzarella cheese
¼	cup chopped fresh parsley
¼	cup thinly sliced green onions
2	tablespoons white wine vinegar
2	teaspoons olive oil
½	teaspoon ground pepper

1. Slice bread in half horizontally. Hollow out center of each half. Set aside hollowed-out halves. Tear inside of bread into small pieces; place in a medium bowl. Add tomato and remaining 6 ingredients; stir well.

2. Spoon tomato mixture into bottom half of bread; top with remaining half. Wrap sandwich in heavy-duty plastic wrap, and chill 8 hours. To serve, slice sandwich into 4 pieces. Yield: 4 servings.

The Italian name of this sandwich means "soaked bread" because the vinaigrette dressing soaks into the baguette halves. Be sure to use a fresh baguette for this recipe; the older the bread, the more difficult it is to slice horizontally. In our kitchens, we prepared the recipe the day we bought the baguette.

SELECTIONS

1 PROTEIN/MILK

3 BREAD

1 FRUIT/VEGETABLE

1 FAT

POINTS

6

PER SERVING

307 CALORIES

45.3G CARBOHYDRATE

7.4G FAT (3.0G SATURATED)

2.8G FIBER

12.6G PROTEIN

15MG CHOLESTEROL

539MG SODIUM

181MG CALCIUM

2.3MG IRON

Round Italian Sandwich *(photo, page 176)*

TIME: PREP 12 MINUTES; CHILL 1 HOUR

SELECTIONS

1 PROTEIN/MILK

2 BREAD

1 FRUIT/VEGETABLE

40 BONUS CALORIES

POINTS

5

PER SERVING

256 CALORIES

34.5G CARBOHYDRATE

7.5G FAT (3.4G SATURATED)

2.6G FIBER

13.7G PROTEIN

24MG CHOLESTEROL

698MG SODIUM

233MG CALCIUM

2.6MG IRON

1   (6½-inch) round loaf sourdough bread (about 8 ounces)
2   (1-ounce) slices provolone cheese
2   slices turkey salami
1   slice turkey ham, halved
2   small tomatoes, thinly sliced
2   cups trimmed arugula or spinach
2   tablespoons balsamic vinegar
2   tablespoons grated Parmesan cheese
½   teaspoon ground pepper

1. Slice bread horizontally into 3 equal layers, using an electric knife or serrated knife. Layer half each of provolone cheese, salami, ham, tomato, and arugula on bottom slice of bread. Sprinkle arugula with half each of balsamic vinegar, Parmesan cheese, and pepper; top with second bread slice. Repeat procedure with remaining provolone cheese, salami, ham, tomato, and arugula. Sprinkle arugula with remaining balsamic vinegar, Parmesan cheese, and pepper; top with remaining bread slice.

2. Wrap sandwich tightly in plastic wrap, and chill 1 hour. To serve, slice sandwich into 4 wedges. Yield: 4 servings.

Tailgaters, take note: Here's the perfect centerpiece for outdoor carry-along meals. Balsamic vinegar and ground pepper make it a deli-style sandwich with upscale flavors. If you can't find a large round sourdough loaf, then layer the filling on small sourdough rolls.

Oriental Beef on Rye

TIME: PREP 9 MINUTES; CHILL 1 HOUR

2   tablespoons nonfat mayonnaise

2   tablespoons low-sodium teriyaki sauce

2   teaspoons peeled, minced gingerroot

1   clove garlic, minced

6   (1-ounce) slices rye bread

½   cup arugula or spinach

2   tablespoons sliced almonds, toasted

9   ounces thinly sliced 98% fat-free deli roast beef

1. Combine first 4 ingredients, mixing well. Spread 1 teaspoon mayonnaise mixture on each of 3 bread slices. Arrange arugula and almonds on top. Drizzle each sandwich with 2 teaspoons mayonnaise mixture. Arrange roast beef evenly on sandwiches. Drizzle each sandwich with 1 teaspoon remaining mayonnaise mixture; top with remaining bread slices. Wrap each sandwich in plastic wrap, and chill at least 1 hour. Yield: 3 servings.

 Ask for custom slices of 98% fat-free deli roast beef at the deli counter in your supermarket.

SELECTIONS

1 PROTEIN/MILK

2 BREAD

40 BONUS CALORIES

POINTS

5

PER SERVING

225 CALORIES

40.4G CARBOHYDRATE

3.8G FAT (0.1G SATURATED)

3.4G FIBER

10.9G PROTEIN

23MG CHOLESTEROL

979MG SODIUM

75MG CALCIUM

1.6MG IRON

Turkey Muffuletta Pita

TIME: PREP 9 MINUTES; CHILL 1 HOUR

SELECTIONS

1 PROTEIN/MILK
1 BREAD
1 FRUIT/VEGETABLE
50 BONUS CALORIES

POINTS

3

PER SERVING

189 CALORIES
22.1G CARBOHYDRATE
5.8G FAT (2.8G SATURATED)
4.4G FIBER
11.1G PROTEIN
22MG CHOLESTEROL
533MG SODIUM
157MG CALCIUM
2.3MG IRON

3	ounces thinly sliced smoked turkey, cut into strips
2	ounces thinly sliced provolone cheese, cut into strips
1½	cups finely chopped sweet red pepper
⅓	cup sliced pimiento-stuffed olives
¼	cup chopped fresh parsley
2	tablespoons fat-free Italian salad dressing
2	tablespoons red wine vinegar
3	small cloves garlic, minced
1	cup shredded iceberg lettuce
2	(6-inch) pita bread rounds, cut in half crosswise

1. Combine first 8 ingredients in a medium bowl; toss well. Cover and chill at least 1 hour.

2. To serve, spoon lettuce evenly into pita halves. Spoon turkey mixture evenly on top of lettuce. Serve immediately. Yield: 4 servings.

Mix up the tangy filling for this pocket sandwich in advance. Then you can stuff the pita halves and serve them in a matter of seconds.

ABOUT THE RECIPES

The recipes featured in this cookbook have been tested following specific guidelines. To achieve similar results, please follow these suggestions:

- When preparing a recipe that yields more than one serving, mix the ingredients well and then divide the mixture evenly into individual portions.

- Where liquid and solid ingredients have to be divided evenly, reserve the liquid, and set it aside. Evenly divide the remaining ingredients; then drizzle equal amounts of the liquid over each serving.

Recipes also include nutritional values per serving for calories, carbohydrate, total fat, saturated fat, fiber, protein, cholesterol, sodium, calcium, and iron. We've abbreviated the measurements as g (grams) and mg (milligrams). The values are based on these assumptions:

- Unless otherwise indicated, meat, poultry, and fish refer to cooked, skinned, and boned servings.

- When we give a range for an ingredient (3 to 3½ cups flour, for instance), we calculate the lesser amount.

- Some alcohol calories evaporate during heating; we reflect that.

- Only the amount of marinade absorbed by the food is calculated.

- Garnishes and optional ingredients are not calculated in the analysis.

The Selections information no longer contains fractions: Bread, Fruit/Vegetable, and Fat are rounded up if 0.5 or above; Protein/Milk is rounded up if 0.75 or above; and only Bonus Calories of 30 or above are listed. If all of the Selections are rounded up, Bonus Calories are decreased; if all of the Selections are rounded down, Bonus Calories are increased.

Recipes include **POINTS** based on Weight Watchers International's 1•2•3 Success Weight Loss Plan. **POINTS** are calculated from a formula based on calories, fat, and fiber that assigns higher points to higher calorie, higher fat foods. Based on your present weight, you are allowed a certain number of **POINTS** per day. (Please turn to page 8 for more information about Selections and **POINTS.)**

RECIPE INDEX

SuperQuick Recipes (15 minutes or less)

Beans and Greens Salad, 139

Black Forest Parfaits, 52

Cranberry-Apple Iced Tea, 23

Easy Parmesan Flounder, 62

Herbed English Peas with Mushrooms, 159

Honey Lamb and Vegetables, 107

Iced Coffee Freeze, 24

Minted Strawberry Soup, 172

Minted Sugar Snaps, 154

Mock Pea Guacamole, 13

Mushroom Pizza Melts, 180

Orange-Scented Couscous Timbales, 168

Parmesan Bruschetta, 26

Sesame Chicken, 126

Sesame Salmon, 65

Smoked Turkey Mango Salad, 146

Strawberry-Cherry Slush, 22

Strawberry Whip, 54

Turkey-Asparagus Roll-Ups, 17

Waldorf Salad, 144

Make-Ahead Recipes

Baked Pita Chips, 12

Basil Chicken and Vegetables, 125

Caramelized Onion Pizza, 80

Chocolate Mousse, 50

Corn Salad, 141

Crème Caramel, 51

Curried Lamb Kabobs, 108

Curry Chicken Salad, 145

Fudgy Brownies, 55

Garlic Herb Cheese Spread, 10

Ginger-Grilled Sirloin Steak, 92

Glazed Citrus Muffins, 30

Grilled Chicken Teriyaki, 113

Herbed Lamb Chops, 110

Key Lime Pie, 49

Lemon Cheesecake, 47

Lemon-Marinated Vegetables, 152

Marinated Mushrooms, 160

Mexican Napa Slaw, 140

Minted Strawberry Soup, 172

Orange Coffee Cake with Streusel
    Topping, 36

Oriental Beef on Rye, 183

Pan Bagna, 181

Poppy Seed Quick Bread, 35

Port Marinated Steaks, 93

Pumpkin Cheesecake, 48

Radish Tartar Sauce, 69

Raisin-Bran Cookies, 56

Raspberry-Orange Yogurt, 53

Red Pepper Pesto Crostini, 14

Round Italian Sandwich, 182

Shrimp Fried Rice, 70

Stir-Fried Brown Rice, 170

Strawberry Bread, 34

Tuna Salad Bites, 18

Turkey-Asparagus Roll-Ups, 17

Turkey Muffuletta Pita, 184

Warm Beef Salad with Figs, 147

White Bean Dip, 11

ACKNOWLEDGMENTS & CREDITS

Aletha Soule, The Loom Co., New York, NY
Annieglass, Watsonville, CA
Carolyn Rice, Marietta, GA
Cyclamen Studio, Inc., Berkeley, CA
Daisy Hill, Louisville, KY
E&M Glass, Cheshire, UK
Eigen Arts, Inc., Jersey City, NJ
Jill Rosenwald, Boston, MA
Karen Alweil Studio, Westminster, CA
Luna Garcia, Venice, CA
Mariposa, Manchester, MA
Mesolini, Bainbridge Island, WI
Pillivyt-Franmara, Salinas, CA
Smyer Glass, Benicia, CA
Vietri, Hillsborough, NC

Contributing photo stylist:
Catherine A. Pittman: pages 115, 117, 135.

Sources of Nutrient Analysis Data: Computrition, Inc.,
Chatsworth, CA, and information
provided by food manufacturers

192

Equivalent Weights & Measures

Food	Weight or Count	Measure or Yield
Apples	1 pound (3 medium)	3 cups sliced
Bananas	1 pound (3 medium)	2⅓ cups sliced or about 2 cups mashed
Bread	about 1½ slices	1 cup soft crumbs
Cabbage	1 pound head	4½ cups shredded
Carrots	1 pound	3 cups shredded
Cottage cheese	16 ounces	2 cups
Chocolate morsels	6-ounce package	1 cup
Coffee	1 pound	80 tablespoons (40 cups perked)
Cookies, vanilla wafers	22 wafers	1 cup finely crushed
Corn	2 medium ears	1 cup kernels
Crackers, graham	14 squares	1 cup fine crumbs
saltine	28 crackers	1 cup finely crushed
Green pepper	1 large	1 cup diced
Lemon	1 medium	2 to 3 tablespoons juice; 2 teaspoons grated rind
Lettuce	1 pound head	6¼ cups torn
Macaroni	4 ounces uncooked (1 cup)	2½ cups cooked
Mushrooms	3 cups whole raw (8 ounces)	1 cup sliced cooked
Oats, quick-cooking	1 cup	1¾ cups cooked
Onion	1 medium	½ cup chopped
Orange	1 medium	⅓ cup juice; 2 tablespoons grated rind
Peaches or Pears	2 medium	1 cup sliced
Potatoes, white	3 medium	2 cups cubed cooked or 1¾ cups mashed
sweet	3 medium	3 cups sliced
Raisins, seedless	16 ounces	3 cups
Rice, long-grain	1 cup uncooked	3 cups cooked
Shrimp, raw in shell	1½ pounds	2 cups (¾ pound) cleaned, cooked
Spaghetti	8 ounces uncooked	4 to 5 cups cooked
Strawberries	1 quart	4 cups sliced
Sugar, powdered	1 pound	3½ cups unsifted
Tomatoes	2½ pounds	3 cups seeded, chopped, and drained